CARIBBEAN

Fiction and Poetry

——

Compiled by
MARJORIE ENGBER

Center for Inter-American Relations
NEW YORK

The Center for Inter-American Relations conducts
educational programs in public affairs, the visual
arts, music, and literature. The Center is a
non-profit, tax-exempt membership corporation,
financed by foundation support, membership dues,
and corporate and individual gifts.

Library of Congress Catalog Card Number 75-147072

Printed in the U.S.A.

Contents

Foreword

This catalog is the second in a series of bibliographies being prepared by the Center for Inter-American Relations. They are designed for students, teachers and scholars interested in contemporary Caribbean and Latin American literature.

The present volume includes works of fiction and poetry by Caribbean authors published in the United States and Great Britain since 1900. We have included from the French-, Dutch- and Spanish-speaking Caribbean only those works that have been translated into English.

The first of the series, *Latin America, Fiction and Poetry in Translation* compiled by Suzanne Jill Levine, included books from Spanish- and Portuguese-speaking countries of the Western Hemisphere published in English in the United States through December 1969. The third volume, dealing with textbooks on Latin American literature, is being prepared by Thomas Colchie.

We hope that this compilation will be useful to those interested in the Caribbean.

José Guillermo Castillo
Director, Literature Program
Center for Inter-American Relations

COMPILER'S NOTES

This catalog includes Caribbean works of fiction and poetry published from 1900 through September 1970.

The country listed after the author's name is in most cases his place of birth and may not be his present place of residence.

An asterisk following the title indicates that the book is out of print. Books are considered out of print according to Bowker's *1969 Books in Print* and *British Books in Print, 1969*, except where more recent information was available. The price of most of the out of print books has been omitted.

Many books in this catalog have been published both in the United States and Great Britain. In such cases, only the American publisher is listed unless the book is out of print in the United States in which case both publishers are listed. Prices quoted in British currency are abbreviated s. (shillings) and d (pence).

Books by the same author are listed in order of publication.

I would like to thank the Reference Departments of the Library of Congress and the Widener Library (Harvard University) for their assistance in this research as well as the Clerk of the Schomberg Collection of the New York Public Library and the personnel of the library at the Research Institute for the Study of Man. I would also like to thank Mrs. Eaulin Ashtine, Senior Library Assistant of the University of the West Indies in Trinidad for the valuable information she provided.

The following works were of particular use in the compilation of this catalog: *West Indian Literature: A Select Bibliography* (The University of the West Indies Library, 1964), *A Bibliography of Caribbean Literature: 1900–1957* by E. Berthe Canton (Current Caribbean Bibliography, Volume 7) and *A Bibliography of Neo-African Literature* by Jahnheinz Jahn (Faber and Faber, London, 1968) which contains a lengthy section on the Caribbean.

M.S.E.

Anthologies

1 *AN ANTHOLOGY OF CONTEMPORARY
LATIN AMERICAN POETRY**
Edited by Dudley Fitts (bilingual edition)
New Directions, Norfolk, 1942. 677 pp. $2.50 (paper)

POETS:

Carmen Alicia Cadilla *Puerto Rico*

Eugenio Florit *Cuba*

Nicolás Guillén *Cuba*

José Lezama Lima *Cuba*

Manuel Muñoz Marín *Puerto Rico*

Luis Palés Matos *Puerto Rico*

Regino Pedroso *Cuba*

Jacques Roumain *Haiti*

Emile Roumer *Haiti*

Duraciné Vaval *Haiti*

TRANSLATORS:

John Peale Bishop, Dudley Fitts, H. R. Hays, Langston Hughes, Muna Lee,
Donald Deverish Walsh.

This anthology also includes works by other Latin American poets.

2 *B.B.C. SHORT STORIES FROM THE B.B.C.
WORLD SERVICE COMPETITION**
British Broadcasting Corporation, London, 1967. 88 pp.

WRITERS:

Clifford Sealy *Trinidad*

John Wickham *Barbados*

This anthology also includes works by other British writers.

3 *THE BEST BRITISH STORIES OF 1928**
Edited by Edward O'Brien
Dodd, Mead and Co., New York, 1928. 335 pp.

WRITERS:

C. L. R. James *Trinidad*

This anthology also includes works by other British writers.

7

4 A BOOK OF BAHAMIAN VERSE*
Selected and edited by Jack Culmer
Bailey, Bros, Ltd., London, 1930. 31 pp.

POETS:

H. C. Christie
Pennington Haile
Richard Kent
Richard Le Gallienne

Julia Warner Michael
Margaret Joyce Scott
Iris Tree

5 CARIBBEAN LITERATURE
Edited and translated by G. R. Coulthard
University of London Press, London, 1966. 128 pp. 15s.
(a collection of prose, poetry and drama)

WRITERS:

George Campbell *Jamaica*
Ernest A. Carr *Trinidad*
Aimé Césaire *Martinique*
Nicolás Guillén *Cuba*
John Hearne *Jamaica*
Errol Hill *Trinidad*
George Lamming *Barbados*
Claude McKay *Jamaica*
René Marqués *Puerto Rico*

Mervyn Morris *Jamaica*
Luis Palés Matos *Puerto Rico*
Eric Roach *Tobago*
Jacques Roumain *Haiti*
Samuel Selvon *Trinidad*
Enrique Serpa *Cuba*
Philip M. Sherlock *Jamaica*
Michael G. Smith *Jamaica*
Derek Walcott *St. Lucia*

6 CARIBBEAN NARRATIVE
Edited by O. R. Dathorne
Heinemann Ltd., London, 1966. 256 pp. 10s 8d, 8s 6d (paper)

WRITERS:

Jan Carew *Guyana*
Neville Dawes *Jamaica*
Herbert De Lisser *Jamaica*
Wilson Harris *Guyana*
John Hearne *Jamaica*
George Lamming *Barbados*
Roger Mais *Jamaica*

Edgar Mittelholzer *Guyana*
V. S. Naipaul *Trinidad*
V. S. Reid *Jamaica*
Andrew Salkey *Jamaica*
Samuel Selvon *Trinidad*
Denis Williams *Guyana*

8

7 *CARIBBEAN PROSE*
Edited by Andrew Salkey
Evans Bros. Ltd., London, 1967. 128 pp. 9s.

WRITERS:

Michael Anthony *Trinidad*
Edward R. Braithwaite *Guyana*
Jan Carew *Guyana*
Neville Dawes *Jamaica*
John Hearne *Jamaica*
C. L. R. James *Trinidad*

George Lamming *Barbados*
Edgar Mittelholzer *Guyana*
Mervyn Morris *Jamaica*
H. Orlando Patterson *Jamaica*
V. S. Reid *Jamaica*
Samuel Selvon *Trinidad*

8 *CARIBBEAN VERSE*
Edited by O. R. Dathorne
William Heinemann Ltd., London, 1967. 144 pp. 9s 6d (paper)

POETS:

Raymond Barrow *British Honduras*
Vera Bell *Jamaica*
George Campbell *Jamaica*
Martin Carter *Guyana*
Frank Collymore *Barbados*
John Figueroa *Jamaica*
A. N. Forde *Grenada*
Wilson Harris *Guyana*
A. L. Hendriks *Jamaica*
C. L. Herbert *Trinidad*
E. McG. Keane *St. Vincent*
George Lamming *Barbados*
W. M. Lawrence *Guyana*
Ian MacDonald *Trinidad*
Basil McFarlane *Jamaica*
C. F. MacIntyre *Jamaica*
Claude McKay *Jamaica*
Roger Mais *Jamaica*
Vera Margon *Jamaica*

Egbert Martin *Guyana*
Stella Mead *Jamaica*
Daisy Myrie *Jamaica*
Alfred Pragnell *Barbados*
Barnabus J. Ramon-Fortuné *Trinidad*
Carl Rattray *Jamaica*
Eric Roach *Tobago*
W. Adolphe Roberts *Jamaica*
Arthur J. Seymour *Guyana*
Philip M. Sherlock *Jamaica*
Michael G. Smith *Jamaica*
Harold Telemaque *Trinidad*
Daniel Thaly *Dominica*
H. A. Vaughan *Barbados*
Vivian Virtue *Jamaica*
Derek Walcott *St. Lucia*
Harold Watson *Jamaica*
Denis Williams *Guyana*

9 *CARIBBEAN VOICES*
(VOLUME I: DREAMS AND VISIONS)
Selected by John Figueroa
Evans Bros. Ltd., London, 1966. 119 pp. 9s. (paper)
(a collection of prose and poetry)

WRITERS:

William Arthur *Barbados*
J. R. Bunting *Jamaica*
George Campbell *Jamaica*
H. D. Carberry *Jamaica*
Jan Carew *Guyana*
Martin Carter *Guyana*
Gilbert de Chambertrand
   Guadeloupe
Frank Collymore *Barbados*
Neville Dawes *Jamaica*
Geoffrey Drayton *Barbados*
Gloria Escoffery *Jamaica*
Barbara Ferland *Jamaica*
John Figueroa *Jamaica*
A. N. Forde *Grenada*
Gilbert Gratiant *Martinique*
G. A. Hamilton *Jamaica*
Vivette Hendriks *Jamaica*
C. L. Herbert *Trinidad*
José María de Heredia *Cuba*
Errol Hill *Trinidad*
Constance Hollar *Jamaica*
Kenneth E. Ingram *Jamaica*
Evan Jones *Jamaica*
Knolly S. La Fortuné *Trinidad*
George Lamming *Barbados*

Archie Lindo *Jamaica*
Mary Lockett *Jamaica*
Edward Lucie-Smith *Jamaica*
Basil McFarlane *Jamaica*
C. F. MacIntyre *U.S.*
Claude McKay *Jamaica*
Roger Mais *Jamaica*
Una Marson *Jamaica*
Stella Mead *Jamaica*
Reginald M. Murray *Jamaica*
Daisy Myrie *Jamaica*
Alfred Pragnell *Barbados*
Barnabus J. Ramon-Fortuné
   Trinidad
Carl Rattray *Jamaica*
Eric Roach *Tobago*
Arthur J. Seymour *Guyana*
Philip M. Sherlock *Jamaica*
Michael G. Smith *Jamaica*
Harold Telemaque *Trinidad*
Daniel Thaly *Dominica*
H. A. Vaughan *Barbados*
Vivian Virtue *Jamaica*
Derek Walcott *St. Lucia*
Harold Watson *Jamaica*
Daniel Williams *St. Vincent*

TRANSLATOR:
C. F. MacIntyre, Vivian Virtue

10 *CARIBBEAN VOICES*
(VOLUME II: THE BLUE HORIZONS)
Selected by John Figueroa
Evans Bros. Ltd., London, 1970. 240 pp. 21s. (paper)
(a collection of prose and poetry)

WRITERS:

Raymond Barrow *British Honduras*
Louise Bennett *Jamaica*
Edward Brathwaite *Barbados*
George Campbell *Jamaica*
H. D. Carberry *Jamaica*
Martin Carter *Guyana*
Frank Collymore *Barbados*
Dennis Craig *Guyana*
Neville Dawes *Jamaica*
Gloria Escoffery *Jamaica*
Barbara Ferland *Jamaica*
John Figueroa *Jamaica*
A. N. Forde *Grenada*
Michael Foster *Barbados*
Albert Gomes *Trinidad*
Cy Grant *Guyana*
Martin Gray
G. A. Hamilton *Jamaica*
Wilson Harris *Guyana*
A. L. Hendriks *Jamaica*
Vivette Hendriks *Jamaica*
C. L. Herbert *Trinidad*
Slade Hopkinson *Guyana*
Kenneth Ingram *Jamaica*
E. McG. Keane *St. Vincent*
George Lamming *Barbados*
Ian McDonald *Trinidad*

Basil McFarlane *Jamaica*
Claude McKay *Jamaica*
Roger Mais *Jamaica*
Una Marson *Jamaica*
Harry Milner *Jamaica*
Edgar Mittelholzer *Guyana*
Mervyn Morris *Jamaica*
Hugh Morrison *Jamaica*
Dorothy Phillips
Alfred Pragnell *Barbados*
Barnabus J. Ramon-Fortuné *Trinidad*
Tom Redcam *Jamaica*
Eric Roach *Tobago*
Andrew Salkey *Jamaica*
Clovis Scott
Dennis Scott *Jamaica*
Michael Scott *Jamaica*
Samuel Selvon *Trinidad*
Arthur J. Seymour *Guyana*
Philip M. Sherlock *Jamaica*
Louis Simpson *Jamaica*
Harold Telemaque *Trinidad*
H. A. Vaughan *Barbados*
Vivian Virtue *Jamaica*
Derek Walcott *St. Lucia*
Daniel Williams *St. Vincent*

11 *CLASSIC TALES FROM SPANISH AMERICA*
Edited, selected and translated by William E. Colford
Barron's Educational Series, Great Neck, 1962. 210 pp. $3.95, $1.50
(paper)

WRITERS:

Cayetano Coll y Toste *Puerto Rico*	Gonzalo Mazas Garbayo *Cuba*
Abelardo Díaz Alfara *Puerto Rico*	Enrique Serpa *Cuba*

This anthology also includes works by other Latin American writers.

12 *COMMONWEALTH POEMS OF TODAY*
Edited by Howard Sergeant
J. Murray, London, 1967. 288 pp. 25s., 10s 6d (paper)

POETS:

Edward Baugh *Jamaica*	Evan Jones *Jamaica*
Edward R. Braithwaite *Guyana*	Edward Lucie-Smith *Jamaica*
Frank Collymore *Barbados*	Ian McDonald *Trinidad*
O. R. Dathorne *Guyana*	Basil McFarlane *Jamaica*
Neville Dawes *Jamaica*	Mervyn Morris *Jamaica*
John Figueroa *Jamaica*	Arthur J. Seymour *Guyana*
A. L. Hendriks *Jamaica*	Louis Simpson *Jamaica*
Slade Hopkinson *Guyana*	Derek Walcott *St. Lucia*

This anthology also includes works by other Commonwealth poets.

13 *CON CUBA: AN ANTHOLOGY OF CUBAN POETRY OF THE LAST SIXTY YEARS*
Edited by Nathaniel Tarn (bilingual edition)
Grossman Publishers, New York, 1969. 144 pp. $4.50, $2.50 (paper)

POETS:

Rafael Alcides	Manuel Díaz Martínez
Orlando Alomá	Eliseo Diego
Miguel Barnet	Froilán Escobar
Victor Casaus	Samuel Feijóo
Belkis Cuza Malé	Lina de Feria

David Fernández
Pablo Armando Fernández
Roberto Fernández Retamar
Gerardo Fulleda León
Fina García Marruz
Félix Guerra
Fayad Jamís
José Lezama Lima
Eduardo Lolo
César López

Luis Marré
Nancy Morejón
Luis Rogelio Nogueras
Pedro de Oraá
Heberto Padilla
Félix Pita Rodríguez
Isel Rivero
Guillermo Rodríguez Rivera
Luis Suardíaz
Cintio Vitier

TRANSLATORS:
Donald Gardner, Carl Hagen, Lionel Kearns, Anthony Kerrigan, Adrian Mitchell, David Ossman, Elinor Randall, Margaret Randall, Tom Raworth Tim Reynolds, Stephen Schwartz.

14 *EBONY RHYTHM: AN ANTHOLOGY OF*
CONTEMPORARY NEGRO VERSE
Edited by Beatrice M. Murphy
The Exposition Press, New York, 1948.
Books for Libraries, Inc., New York, 1968. 161 pp. $6.50

POETS:
Jean Brierre *Haiti*
Edna L. Harrison *Jamaica*
Eldon George McLean *Trinidad*

Edward Richards *St. Thomas*
Ricardo Weeks *Puerto Rico*

TRANSLATOR:
J. F. Matheus.

15 *THE FLUTE, WITH OTHER TRANSLATIONS*
AND A POEM*
Edited and translated by Herbert John Clifford Grierson
Samson Press, Warlinghame, U.K., 1931. 36 pp.

WRITERS:
José María de Heredia *Cuba*

This anthology also includes works by other Latin American writers.

16 *FROM THE GREEN ANTILLES**
Edited by Barbara Howes
Macmillan, New York, 1966. 368 pp. $6.95
(a selection of prose and poetry)

WRITERS:

Emilio S. Belaval *Puerto Rico*
Tomás Blanco *Puerto Rico*
Juan Bosch *Dominican Republic*
Lydia Cabrera *Cuba*
Alejo Carpentier *Cuba*
Aimé Césaire *Martinique*
Gilbert de Chambertrand *Guadeloupe*
Austin C. Clarke *Barbados*
Frank A. Collymore *Barbados*
Cola Debrot *Bonaire*
Abelardo Díaz Alfaro *Puerto Rico*
Eliseo Diego *Cuba*
Pierre Duprey *Martinique*
A. N. Forde *Grenada*
Nicolás Guillén *Cuba*
John Hearne *Jamaica*
Albert Helman *Surinam*
Daniel Samaroo Joseph *Trinidad*
Ismith Khan *Trinidad*
George Lamming *Barbados*

Boeli van Leeuwen *Netherlands Antilles*
Magloire-Saint-Aude *Haiti*
Roger Mais *Jamaica*
Tip Marugg *Curaçao*
Carlos Montenegro *Cuba*
Florette Morand *Guadeloupe*
V. S. Naipaul *Trinidad*
Lino Novás Calvo *Cuba*
V. S. Reid *Jamaica*
Clément Richer *Martinique*
René de Rooy *Surinam-Curaçao*
St.-John Perse *Guadeloupe*
Karl Sealey *Barbados*
Samuel Selvon *Trinidad*
Pedro Juan Soto *Puerto Rico*
Raphaël Tardon *Martinique*
Philippe Thoby-Marcelin *Haiti*
Derek Walcott *St. Lucia*
Joseph Zobel *Martinique*

TRANSLATORS:

Lionel Abel, Hubert van den Bergh, Patrick Bowles, Alex Brotherton, Estelle Reed Debrot, Roy Edwards, Frances Frenaye, Langston Hughes, Merloyd Lawrence, Joan Maclean, Zoila Nelken, Harriet de Onís, Frances Willard von Maltitz, R. R. Symonds, Eva Thoby-Marcelin, Nick Vandemoer, Louise Varèse.

17 *THE GOLDEN LAND: AN ANTHOLOGY OF*
LATIN AMERICAN FOLKLORE IN LITERATURE*
Selected, edited and translated by Harriet de Onís
Knopf, New York, 1948. 395 pp.
(a selection of short stories)

WRITER:
Gertrudis Gómez de Avellaneda
Cuba

This anthology also includes works by other Latin American writers.

18 *GROUP OF TRANSLATIONS OF*
AMERICAN VERSE*
Translated by Alice Stone Blackwell (bilingual edition)
Pan American Union, Washington, D.C., 1928. 7 pp.

POET:
Enrique Hernández Miyares *Cuba*

This anthology also includes works by other Latin American writers.

19 *HISPANIC ANTHOLOGY: POEMS TRANSLATED*
FROM THE SPANISH BY ENGLISH AND
NORTH AMERICAN POETS*
Edited by Thomas Walsh (bilingual edition)
Putnam, New York, 1920. 779 pp.

POETS:

Mariano Brull *Cuba*	Muna Lee de Muñoz Marín
Julián del Casal *Cuba*	*Puerto Rico*
Virgilio Dávila *Puerto Rico*	René López *Cuba*
Fabio Fiallo *Dominican Republic*	Rafael María de Mendive *Cuba*
Gertrudis Gómez de Avellaneda	Luis Muñoz Rivera *Puerto Rico*
Cuba	Ramón Domingo Perés *Cuba*
José María de Heredia *Cuba*	Antonio Pérez-Pierret *Puerto Rico*
Enrique Hernández Miyares *Cuba*	Martina Pierra de Poo *Cuba*

Plácido *Cuba*
José Manuel Poveda *Cuba*
Lola Rodríguez del Tío *Puerto Rico*

Antonio Sellén *Cuba*
Diego Vicente Tejera *Cuba*

TRANSLATORS:
Joseph Clarke, Alfred Coester, Roderick Gill, Jorge Godoy, Muna Lee, H. W. Longfellow, Garrett Strange, Thomas Walsh.

20 *INTRODUCTION 2; STORIES BY NEW WRITERS*
Faber and Faber, London, 1964. 187 pp. 21s.

WRITER:
Garth St. Omer *St. Lucia*

This anthology also includes works by other British writers

21 *ISLAND VOICES: STORIES FROM THE WEST INDIES*
Edited by Andrew Salkey
Liveright, New York, 1970. 256 pp. $4.95

WRITERS:
Michael Anthony *Trinidad*
Edward R. Braithwaite *Guyana*
Jan Carew *Guyana*
O. R. Dathorne *Guyana*
A. N. Forde *Grenada*
Cecil Gray *Jamaica*
John Hearne *Jamaica*
Donald Hinds *Jamaica*

C. L. R. James *Trinidad*
George Lamming *Barbados*
V. S. Naipaul *Trinidad*
H. Orlando Patterson *Jamaica*
R. O. Robinson *Jamaica*
Samuel Selvon *Trinidad*
Claude Thompson *Jamaica*
Denis Williams *Guyana*

22 *LATIN AMERICAN WRITING TODAY*
Edited by J. M. Cohen
Penguin Books, Baltimore, 1967. 267 pp. $3.25 (paper)

WRITERS:

Guillermo Cabrera Infante *Cuba*   Alejo Carpentier *Cuba*
Onelio Jorge Cardoso *Cuba*   Pablo Armando Fernández *Cuba*

TRANSLATORS:

Arthur Boyars, J. G. Brotherston, Jean Franco, John Gibson, Christopher Middleton.

This anthology also includes works by other Latin American writers.

23 *THE LITERATURE OF LATIN AMERICA*
*(VOLUME I)**
Pan American Union, Washington, D.C., 1944. 64 pp.

WRITERS:

Antonio Nicolás Blanco *Puerto*   Frédéric Marcelin *Haiti*
   Rico   José Martí *Cuba*
José María de Heredia *Cuba*

TRANSLATOR:

Muna Lee.

24 *MODERN POETRY FROM SPAIN AND*
LATIN AMERICA
Translated by Nan Braymer and Lillian Lowenfels
Corinth Books, New York, 1964. 63 pp. $1.45 (paper)

POET:

Nicolás Guillén *Cuba*

This anthology also includes works by other authors from Spain and Latin America.

25 MUSA BILINGÜE*

Edited by Francisco Javier Amy (bilingual edition)
Boletín Mercantil, San Juan, 1903. 329 pp.

POETS:

Francisco Javier Amy *Puerto Rico*
José Gautier-Benítez *Puerto Rico*
José María de Heredia *Cuba*
Rafael María de Mendive *Cuba*

José Jacinto Milanés *Cuba*
Francisco Sellén *Cuba*
Juan Clemente Zenee *Cuba*

TRANSLATORS:

Francisco Javier Amy, William Cullen Bryant, L. E. Levy.

26 NÉGRITUDE: BLACK POETRY FROM AFRICA AND THE CARIBBEAN

Edited and translated by Norman R. Shapiro (bilingual edition)
October House, Inc., New York, 1970. 240 pp. $7.50, $2.95 (paper)

POETS:

Jean Brierre *Haiti*
Carl Brouard *Haiti*
Roussan Camille *Haiti*
Aimé Césaire *Martinique*
Henri Corbin *Guadeloupe*
Léon Damas *French Guiana*
René Depestre *Haiti*
Auguste Desportes *Martinique*
Joselyn Etienne *Guadeloupe*
Gilbert Gratiant *Martinique*

Gabrielle Jos *Guadeloupe*
Léon Laleau *Haiti*
Frantz Leroy *Haiti*
Rudolph Moise *Haiti*
Paul E. Najac *Haiti*
Louis Neptune *Haiti*
Anthony Phelps *Haiti*
René Philoctete *Haiti*
Joseph Polius *Martinique*
Marie-Thérèse Rouil *Martinique*

This anthology also includes works by African poets.

27 *NEW VOICES OF HISPANIC AMERICA;*
    AN ANTHOLOGY*
Edited and translated by Darwin J. Flakoll and Claribel Alegría
Beacon Press, Boston, 1962. 226 pp.
(selections of fiction and poetry, including original text of poems)

WRITERS:

Fayad Jamís *Cuba*   Nivaria Tejera *Cuba*
René Marqués *Puerto Rico*   Cintio Vitier *Cuba*

This anthology also includes works by other Latin American
authors.

28 *NEW VOICES OF THE COMMONWEALTH*
Edited by Howard Sergeant
Evans Bros. Ltd., London, 1968. 208 pp. 30s., 12s. (paper)

WRITERS:

Edward Baugh *Jamaica*   Ian McDonald *Trinidad*
Edward R. Braithwaite *Guyana*   Basil McFarlane *Jamaica*
Frank Collymore *Barbados*   Mervyn Morris *Jamaica*
O. R. Dathorne *Guyana*   Eric Roach *Tobago*
Neville Dawes *Jamaica*   Karl Sealey *Barbados*
A. L. Hendriks *Jamaica*   Arthur J. Seymour *Guyana*
Slade Hopkinson *Guyana*   Louis Simpson *Jamaica*
Evan Jones *Jamaica*   Vivian Virtue *Jamaica*
Cliff Lashley *Jamaica*   Derek Walcott *St. Lucia*
Edward Lucie-Smith *Jamaica*

This anthology also includes works by other Commonwealth
writers.

29 *NINE LATIN AMERICAN POETS*
Edited and translated by Rachel Benson (bilingual edition)
Las Americas, New York, 1968. 359 pp. $6.50

POET:
Luis Palés Matos *Puerto Rico*

This anthology also includes works by other Latin American poets.

30 *THE ODES OF BELLO, OLMEDO AND HEREDIA**
Edited and translated by Elijah G. Hills
G. P. Putnam's, New York, 1920. 153 pp.

POET:
José María de Heredia *Cuba*

This anthology also includes works by other Latin American authors.

31 *OUR WORD: GUERILLA POEMS FROM*
LATIN AMERICA
Translated by Edward Dorn and Gordon Brotherston (bilingual edition)
Grossman Publishers, New York, 1968. 76 pp. $4.50, $2.95 (paper)

POETS:
Pablo Hernando Guerrero *Cuba*   Che Guevara *Cuba*

This anthology also includes works by other Latin American poets.

32 *PAN AMERICAN POEMS, AN ANTHOLOGY**
Compiled by Agnes Blake Poor
The Gorham Press, Boston, 1918. 80 pp.

POETS:
José de Diego *Puerto Rico*   José María de Heredia *Cuba*
Gertrudis Gómez de Avellaneda
Cuba

TRANSLATORS:
William Cullen Bryant, Agnes Blake Poor.

This anthology also includes works by other Latin American poets.

33 *THE PENGUIN BOOK OF SPANISH VERSE**
Edited and translated by John Michael Cohen (bilingual edition with
    plain prose translations)
Penguin Books, Baltimore, 1956. 441 pp.

POET:
Nicolás Guillén *Cuba*

This anthology also includes works by other Spanish and Latin
American poets.

34 *PENGUIN MODERN POETS 6*
Penguin Books, Harmondsworth, U.K., 1964. 124 pp. 3s 6d (paper)

POET:
Edward Lucie-Smith *Jamaica*

This anthology also includes works by other English poets.

35 *PENGUIN MODERN STORIES 1*
Edited by Judith Burnley
Penguin Books, Harmondsworth, U.K., 1969. 115 pp. 4s. (paper)

WRITER:
Jean Rhys *Dominica*

This anthology also includes works by other English writers.

36 *PENGUIN MODERN STORIES 4*

Edited by Judith Burnley

Penguin Books, Harmondsworth, U.K., 1970. 142 pp. 4s. (paper)

WRITER:

Shiva Naipaul *Trinidad*

This anthology also includes works by other English writers.

37 *THE POETRY OF THE NEGRO, 1746–1949**

Edited by Langston Hughes and Arna Bontemps

Doubleday, New York, 1949. 429 pp.

POETS:

Jean Brierre *Haiti*
Roussan Camille *Haiti*
George Campbell *Jamaica*
H. D. Carberry *Jamaica*
Aimé Césaire *Martinique*
Frank A. Collymore *Barbados*
Léon Damas *French Guiana*
Oswald Durand *Haiti*
Luc Grimard *Haiti*
Nicolás Guillén *Cuba*
Constance Hollar *Jamaica*
Kenneth E. Ingram *Jamaica*
Basil McFarlane *Jamaica*
John E. C. McFarlane *Jamaica*
Claude McKay *Jamaica*
Roger Mais *Jamaica*
Una Marson *Jamaica*
Agnes Maxwell-Hall *Jamaica*
Louis Morpeau *Haiti*
Ignace Nau *Haiti*

Stephanie Ormsby *Jamaica*
Regino Pedroso *Cuba*
Plácido *Cuba*
Charles F. Pressoir *Haiti*
Tom Redcam *Jamaica*
W. Adolphe Roberts *Jamaica*
Jacques Roumain *Haiti*
Emile Roumer *Haiti*
Arthur J. Seymour *Guyana*
Philip M. Sherlock *Jamaica*
Louis Simpson *Jamaica*
Normil Sylvain *Haiti*
Harold Telemaque *Trinidad*
Philippe Thoby-Marcelin *Haiti*
Isaac Toussaint-L'Ouverture *Haiti*
H. A. Vaughan *Barbados*
Duraciné Vaval *Haiti*
Vivian Virtue *Jamaica*
Christian Werleigh *Haiti*

TRANSLATORS:

Lionel Abel, John Peale Bishop, Ben F. Carruthers, Mercer Cook, Ivan Goll. Langston Hughes, James Weldon Johnson, John F. Matheus, Edna W. Underwood, Donald Devenish Walsh.

38 *THE POETS OF HAITI, 1782–1934**
Edited and translated by Edna W. Underwood
The Mosher Press, Portland, 1934. 159 pp.

POETS:

Macdonald Alexander
Fernand Ambroise
Louis Borno
Jean Brierre
Carl Brouard
Frédéric Burr-Reynaud
Adrian Carrénard
Maurice Casséus
Pascal Casséus
Roland Chassagne
Arsène Chevry
Massilon Coicou
Louis-Henri Durand
Oswald Durand
Luc Grimard
Tertullien Guilbaud
Dominique Hippolyte
Edmund La Forest
Léon Laleau
Robert Lataillade
George Lescouflair
Paul Lochard
Léon Louhis
Clément Magloire-Fils

Victor Mangonés
Constantin Mayard
Pierre Mayard
Charles Moravia
Louis Morpeau
Ignace Nau
Edgard Numa
Timothée Paret
Charles F. Pressoir
Christian Regulies
Justinien Ricot
Volvick Ricourt
Milo Rigaud
Jacques Roumain
Emile Roumer
George Sylvain
Normil Sylvain
Philippe Thoby-Marcelin
Isaac Toussaint-L'Ouverture
Duraciné Vaval
Damoclès Vieux
Etzer Vilaire
Jean-Joseph Vilaire
Christian Werleigh

39 *PRIZE STORIES FROM LATIN AMERICA*
Winners of the *Life en Español* Literary Contest
Doubleday paperback, New York, 1964. 383 pp. $1.45

WRITERS:
Ramón Ferreira López *Cuba*   Faustino González-Aller *Cuba*

TRANSLATORS:
Paul Blackburn, Izaak A. Langnas.

This anthology also includes works by other authors.

40 *PUERTO RICO. LA NUEVA VIDA. THE NEW LIFE*
Edited by Nina Kaiden, Pedro Juan Soto and Andrew Vladimir
  (bilingual edition)
Renaissance Editions (Corinthian Editions Inc.), New York, 1966.
  80 pp. $5.00
(a selection of prose, poetry and art)

WRITERS:

Margot Arce de Vazquez
Guillermo Atiles García
María Teresa Babin
Emilio S. Belaval
Tomás Blanco
Julia de Burgos
Carmen Alicia Cadilla
Juan Antonio Corretjer
Emilio Díaz Valcarcel
José de Diego
Edwin Figueroa
José Luis González
José P. H. Hernández

Luis Hernández Aquino
José de Jesús Esteves
Clara Lair
Luis Llorens Torres
Salvador M. de Jesús
Hugo Margenat
Ramón Julia Marín
René Marqués
Luis Muñoz Rivera
Luis Palés Matos
Carmen Puigdollers
Pedro Juan Soto

TRANSLATORS:

Charles Connelly, Nina Kaiden, Lysander Kemp, C. Virginia Matters,
Georgina Pando, Charles Pilditch, Patricia Vallés.

·**41** *RESPONSE*
Edited by Cecil Gray
Nelson and Sons, London, 1969. 192 pp. 8s. (paper)

WRITERS:

Michael Anthony *Trinidad*
Timothy Callender *Barbados*
A. N. Forde *Grenada*
Bernard Graham *Barbados*
Cecil Gray *Jamaica*
Paul Layne *Barbados*
Robert Lucas

Louis Marriott *Jamaica*
Edgar Mittelholzer *Guyana*
Millicent Payne *Barbados*
Barnabus J. Ramon-Fortuné
  Trinidad
V. S. Reid *Jamaica*
Clifford Sealey *Trinidad*

Monica Skeete *Barbados*   N. E. Timothy
Flora Squires *Barbados*   F. D. Weller *Jamaica*

42 *SHORT STORIES OF LATIN AMERICA**
Edited by Arturo Torres-Rioseco
Translated by Zoila Nelken and Rosalie Torres-Rioseco
Las Americas, New York, 1963. 203 pp. $3.50

WRITERS:

Alejo Carpentier *Cuba*   Félix Pita Rodríguez *Cuba*
Lino Novás Calvo *Cuba*

This anthology also includes works by other Latin American
authors.

43 *SOME SPANISH AMERICAN POETS*
Edited by Isaac Goldberg
Translated by Alice Stone Blackwell (bilingual edition)
Greenwood Press, New York, 1968. 559 pp. $19.50

POETS:

Dulce María Borrero de Luján   José María de Heredia *Cuba*
   Cuba   Enrique Hernández Miyares *Cuba*
Bonifacio Byrne *Cuba*   Concha Meléndez *Puerto Rico*
José Gautier Bénitez *Puerto Rico*   Ramón de Palma y Romay *Cuba*
Gertrudis Gómez de Avellaneda
   Cuba

This anthology also includes works by other Latin American
authors.

44 *SPANISH AMERICAN LITERATURE IN TRANSLATION. VOLUME I*
Edited by Willis K. Jones
Frederick Ungar, New York, 1963. 356 pp. $7.50
(a selection of prose, poetry and drama before 1888)

WRITERS:

Manuel de Jésus Galvan *Dominican Republic*

José Gautier Benítez *Puerto Rico*

Gertrudis Gómez de Avellaneda *Cuba*

José María de Heredia *Cuba*

Joaquín Lorenzo Luaces *Cuba*

José Jacinto Milanés y Fuentes *Cuba*

Juan Gualberto Padilla *Puerto Rico*

Plácido *Cuba*

Cirilo Villaverde *Cuba*

TRANSLATORS:

Prose: Willis K. Jones.

Poetry: Read Bain, William Cullen Bryant, H. W. Hurlbut, Willis K. Jones.

This anthology also includes works by other Latin American writers.

45 *SPANISH AMERICAN LITERATURE IN TRANSLATION. VOLUME II*
Edited by Willis K. Jones
Frederick Ungar, New York, 1963. 469 pp. $8.50
(a selection of prose, poetry and drama since 1888)

WRITERS:

Julián del Casal *Cuba*

Nicolás Guillén *Cuba*

Enrique Hernández Miyares *Cuba*

Luis Llorens Torres *Puerto Rico*

José Martí *Cuba*

Luis Palés Matos *Puerto Rico*

Regino Pedroso *Cuba*

Cesáreo Rosa-Nieves *Puerto Rico*

TRANSLATORS:

Alice Stone Blackwell, Ben F. Carruthers, Joseph Leonard Grucci, Langston Hughes, Willis K. Jones, Muna Lee, Thomas Walsh.

This anthology also includes works by other Latin American writers.

46 *SPANISH AMERICAN POETRY:*
A BILINGUAL SELECTION
Compiled by Seymour Resnick
Harvey House, Irvington-on-Hudson, 1964. 96 pp. $3.50

POETS:

Fabio Fiallo *Dominican Republic*   José María de Heredia *Cuba*
Gertrudis Gómez de Avellaneda   José Martí *Cuba*
   Cuba   Plácido *Cuba*

TRANSLATORS:
Alice Stone Blackwell, William Cullen Bryant, Seymour Resnick.

This anthology also includes works by other Latin American poets.

47 *SPANISH STORIES AND TALES**
Edited by Harriet de Onís
Knopf, New York, 1954. 270 pp. $3.95

WRITER:
Lino Novás Calvo *Cuba*

TRANSLATOR:
Raymond Sayers

This anthology also includes workes by other Spanish and Latin
   American writers.

48 *STORIES FROM THE CARIBBEAN*
Edited by Andrew Salkey
Dufour, Philadelphia, 1965. 256 pp. $6.00

WRITERS:

Michael Anthony *Trinidad*   A. N. Forde *Grenada*
Edward R. Braithwaite *Guyana*   Cecil Gray *Trinidad*
Jan Carew *Guyana*   John Hearne *Jamaica*
Oscar R. Dathorne *Guyana*   Donald Hinds *Jamaica*

C. L. R. James *Trinidad*
George Lamming *Barbados*
Edgar Mittelholzer *Guyana*
V. S. Naipaul *Trinidad*
H. Orlando Patterson *Jamaica*

R. O. Robinson *Jamaica*
Samuel Selvon *Trinidad*
Claude Thompson *Jamaica*
Denis Williams *Guyana*

49 *THE SUN'S EYE:*
WEST INDIAN WRITING FOR YOUNG READERS
Compiled by Anne Walmsley
Longmans, Green and Co., London, 1968. 144 pp. 6s 9d.

WRITERS:

Michael Anthony *Trinidad*
Edward R. Braithwaite *Guyana*
Timothy Callendar *Barbados*
H. D. Carberry *Jamaica*
Jan Carew *Guyana*
Martin Carter *Guyana*
Frank Collymore *Barbados*
Neville Dawes *Jamaica*
Geoffrey Drayton *Barbados*
Wilson Harris *Guyana*
John Hearne *Jamaica*
A. L. Hendriks *Jamaica*
Kenneth Ingram *Jamaica*
Evan Jones *Jamaica*
George Lamming *Barbados*

Lauchmonen *Guyana*
Edward Lucie-Smith *Jamaica*
Roger Mais *Jamaica*
Agnes Maxwell-Hall *Jamaica*
Ralph Prince *Antigua*
V. S. Reid *Jamaica*
Eric Roach *Tobago*
Namba Roy *Jamaica*
Andrew Salkey *Jamaica*
Dennis Scott *Jamaica*
Samuel Selvon *Trinidad*
Arthur J. Seymour *Guyana*
Philip M. Sherlock *Jamaica*
Derek Walcott *St. Lucia*
F. D. Weller *Jamaica*

50 *SWAN, CYGNETS, AND OWL;*
AN ANTHOLOGY OF MODERNIST POETRY IN
*SPANISH AMERICA**
Edited and translated by Mildred E. Johnson
The University of Missouri Studies, Columbia, 1956. 199 pp. $4.00
(paper)

POETS:
Julián del Casal *Cuba*   José Martí *Cuba*

This anthology also includes works by other Latin American poets.

51 *A TREASURY OF JAMAICAN POETRY**
Selected and edited by John E. C. McFarlane
University of London Press, London, 1949. 159 pp.

POETS:

George Campbell
H. D. Carberry
Astley Clerk
H. Gillies Clerk
M. V. Clerk
Stanley Fyffe
Clara Maud Garrett
Faith Goodheart
Constance Hollar
Ruth Hornor
Albinia C. Hutton
Kenneth E. Ingram
P. M. Myers Johnson
Lena Kent
Mary Lockett
W. O. MacDonald
Basil McFarlane
John E. C. McFarlane
Claude McKay
Roger Mais

Una Marson
Agnes Maxwell-Hall
Arabel Moulton-Barrett
G. McKenzie Muir
Reginald M. Murray
Arthur E. Nicholas
Eva R. Nicholas
Stephanie Ormsby
Tom Redcam
W. Adolphe Roberts
Philip M. Sherlock
Michael G. Smith
Claude Thompson
Tropica
V. M. C.
Vivian L. Virtue
R. Warren
Harold Watson
Dorothy Whitfield

52 *THE TRIQUARTERLY ANTHOLOGY OF
CONTEMPORARY LATIN AMERICAN LITERATURE*
Edited by José Donoso and William Henkin
Dutton, New York, 1969. 496 pp. $8.95, $3.95 (paper)

WRITERS:

Miguel Barnet *Cuba*
Eliseo Diego *Cuba*
Pablo Armando Fernández *Cuba*
Roberto Fernández Retamar *Cuba*

Fayad Jamís *Cuba*
José Lezama Lima *Cuba*
Heberto Padilla *Cuba*

TRANSLATORS:
Elinor Randall, Margaret Randall, Tim Reynolds.

This anthology also includes works by other Latin American authors.

53 *TWELVE SPANISH AMERICAN POETS: AN ANTHOLOGY**
Edited and translated by H. R. Hays (bilingual edition)
Yale University Press, New Haven, 1943. 336 pp.

POETS:

Eugenio Florit *Cuba*   Nicolás Guillén *Cuba*

This anthology also includes works by other Latin American poets.

54 *VOICES FROM SUMMERLAND; AN ANTHOLOGY OF JAMAICAN POETRY**
Edited by John E. C. McFarlane
Fowler Wright, London, 1929. 307 pp.

POETS:

Astley Clerk   Arabel Mounton-Barrett
H. Gillies Clerk   G. McKenzie Muir
Constance Hollar   Phyllis May Myers
Thomas H. MacDermot   Arthur E. Nicholas
John E. C. McFarlane   W. Adolphe Roberts
Claude McKay

55 *WEST INDIAN NARRATIVE: AN INTRODUCTORY ANTHOLOGY*
Edited by Kenneth Ramchand
Humanities Press, New York, 1966. 221 pp. $2.00 (paper)

WRITERS:

Michael Anthony *Trinidad*   Jan Carew *Guyana*
Edward R. Braithwaite *Guyana*   Herbert G. De Lisser *Jamaica*

Geoffrey Drayton *Barbados*
Wilson Harris *Guyana*
John Hearne *Jamaica*
C. L. R. James *Trinidad*
George Lamming *Barbados*
Claude McKay *Jamaica*
Roger Mais *Jamaica*

Edgar Mittelholzer *Guyana*
V. S. Naipaul *Trinidad*
V. S. Reid *Jamaica*
Namba Roy *Jamaica*
Andrew Salkey *Jamaica*
Samuel Selvon *Trinidad*

56 *WEST INDIAN STORIES*
Edited by Andrew Salkey
Faber and Faber, London, 1960. 224 pp. 7s 6d (paper)

WRITERS:

Edward R. Braithwaite *Guyana*
Jan Carew *Guyana*
Geoffrey Drayton *Barbados*
John Figueroa *Jamaica*
Stuart Hall *Jamaica*
Wilson Harris *Guyana*
John Hearne *Jamaica*
A. L. Hendriks *Jamaica*
Roy Henry *Jamaica*

George Lamming *Barbados*
Roger Mais *Jamaica*
Edgar Mittelholzer *Guyana*
Barnabus J. Ramon-Fortuné
    Trinidad
V. S. Reid *Jamaica*
Karl Sealey *Barbados*
Samuel Selvon *Trinidad*
Jan Williams *Trinidad*

57 *WRITERS IN THE NEW CUBA*
Edited by J. M. Cohen
Penguin Books, Baltimore, 1967. 191 pp. $3.25 (paper)

WRITERS:

Luis Agüero
Domingo Alfonso
José Alvarez Baragaño
Humberto Arenal
Antón Arrufat
Guillermo Cabrera Infante
Onelio Jorge Cardoso
Calvert Casey

Fidel Castro
Jesús Díaz Rodríguez
Abelardo Estorino
Pablo Armando Fernández
Roberto Fernández Retamar
Reynaldo González
Fayad Jamís
Rogelio Llopis

Luis Marré

Heberto Padilla

Virgilio Piñera

Rolando Rigali

Ana María Simo

TRANSLATORS:
J. G. Brotherston, J. M. Cohen, Jean Franco.

58 *YOUNG COMMONWEALTH POETRY**
Edited by Peter Ludwig Brent
William Heinemann Ltd., London, 1965. 216 pp. 12s.

POETS:

Edward R. Braithwaite *Guyana*

Jan Carew *Guyana*

Martin Carter *Guyana*

O. R. Dathorne *Guyana*

Neville Dawes *Jamaica*

A. N. Forde *Grenada*

A. L. Hendriks *Jamaica*

C. L. Herbert *Trinidad*

Evan Jones *Jamaica*

Ellsworth Keane *St. Vincent*

George Lamming *Barbados*

Edward Lucie-Smith *Jamaica*

Mervyn Morris *Jamaica*

Eric M. Roach *Tobago*

Dennis Scott *Jamaica*

Derek Walcott *St. Lucia*

This anthology also includes works by other Commonwealth poets

Poetry

59 Allfrey, Phyllis Shand *Domincia*
IN CIRCLES, POEMS*
The Raven Press, Harrow Weald, Middlesex, U.K., 1940. 20 pp.

60 Anduze, Aubrey A. *St. Thomas*
REMINISCENCE*
The Art Shop, St. Thomas, 1940. 39 pp.

61 Bennett, Henry Charles *Jamaica*
THIRTEEN POEMS AND SEVEN*
Edgar G. Dunsten and Co., London, 1935. 45 pp.

62 Blackman, Peter *Jamaica*
MY SONG IS FOR ALL MEN*
International Publishers, New York, 1952. 20 pp.

63 Brathwaite, Edward *Barbados*
RIGHTS OF PASSAGE
Oxford University Press, New York, 1967. 86 pp. $3.75

64 Brathwaite, Edward
MASKS
Oxford University Press, New York, 1968 80 pp. $4.25

65 Brathwaite, Edward
ISLANDS
Oxford University Press, New York, 1969. 113 pp. $3.75

66 Brown, Paula *St. John*
A WOMAN SINGING, POEMS AND DRAWINGS*
Cruz Bay Arts, St. John, 1958. 64 pp.

67 Carter, Martin *Guyana*
POEMS OF RESISTANCE FROM BRITISH GUIANA*
Lawrence and Wishart, London, 1954. 20 pp. 1s 6d (paper)

67a Casal, Julián del *Cuba*
SELECTED POEMS
University of Alabama Press, University, 1949. 140 pp. $2.00 (paper)

68 Césaire, Aimé *Martinique*
RETURN TO MY NATIVE LAND
Translated by John Berger and Anna Bostock
Penguin Books, Harmondsworth, U.K., 1969. 95 pp. $0.95 (paper)
(original title: *Cahier d'un retour au pays natal*)

69 Combs, Tram *St. Thomas*
PILGRIM'S TERRACE: POEMS*
Editorial La Nueva Salamanca, San Juan, 1957. 86 pp.

70 Combs, Tram
CEREMONIES IN MIND;
ARTISTS, BOYS, CATS, LOVERS, JUDGES, PRIESTS*
The Art Shop, St. Thomas, 1959. 30 pp.

71 Combs, Tram
BUT NEVER MIND; POEMS 1946–1950*
Golden Mountain Press, San Francisco, 1961. Unpaged.

72 Combs, Tram
SAINT THOMAS, POEMS
Weslyan University Press, Middletown, 1965. 83 pp. $4.00, $2.00
(paper)

73 Combs, Tram
BRIEFS; POEMS*
Hillside Press, Franklin, 1966. 80 pp.

74 Creque, Cyril F. W. *Charlotte Amalie*
TRADE WINDS*
Franklin Printing House, Newport, 1934. 110 pp.

75 Creque, Cyril F. W.
PANORAMA; ST. THOMAS, VIRGIN ISLANDS.
POEMS*
Kenyon Press Publishing Co., Wauwatosa, 1947. 81 pp.

76 Damas, Léon *French Guiana*
AFRICAN SONGS OF LOVE, WAR, GRIEF AND ABUSE*
Translated by Miriam Koshland and Ulli Beier
Northwestern University Press, Evanston, 1963. 40 pp. $1.75 (paper)
(original title not available)

77 Daniel, Edith *Trinidad*
GEMS IN VERSE*
Arthur Stockwell, Ilfracombe, Devon, U.K., 1962. 19 pp.

78 Dávila, Virgilio *Puerto Rico*
OBRAS COMPLETAS. COMPLETE WORKS*
Instituto de Cultura Puertorriqueña, San Juan, 1964. 614 pp.
(English translations of some of the poems)

79 Dávila, Virgilio
PUEBLITO DE ANTES
Translated by José Antonio Dávila (bilingual edition)
Editorial Cordillera, San Juan, 1967, 99 pp.

80 De Laney, Lessie A. *Trinidad*
VERSES FROM THE CARIBBEAN*
Arthur Stockwell, Ilfracombe, Devon, U.K., no date. 24 pp.

81 Drayton, Geoffrey *Barbados*
THREE MERIDIANS*
Ryerson Press, Toronto, 1950. 8 pp.

82 Figueroa, John *Jamaica*
LOVE LEAPS HERE*
Tinling, Liverpool, 1962. 60 pp.

83 Gimenez, J. P. *St Thomas*
*THE VIRGIN ISLANDS FOLKLORE AND OTHER
    POEMS**
Harding, New York, 1933. 103 pp.

84 Gimenez, J. P.
CARIBBEAN ECHOES*
Galleon Press, New York, 1934. 62 pp.

85 Gimenez, J. P.
DEEP WATERS*
The Art Shop, St. Thomas, 1939. 72 pp.

86 Gimenez, J. P.
VOICE OF THE VIRGIN ISLAND'S MYSTIC POET*
Dorrance and Co., Philadelphia, 1952. 50 pp.

87 Giraudier, Antonio *Cuba*
GREEN AGAINST LINEN AND OTHER POEMS*
Translated by Antonio Giraudier and Samuel Weisberg
Bookman Associates, New York, 1957. 89 pp.

88 Giraudier, Antonio
*RAINSWILL**
Anonymous translation
Dorrance and Co., Philadelphia, 1962. 59 pp.
(a selection of poetry with some prose)

89 Giraudier, Antonio
*POETICAL NOTES FOR 24 COLLAGES**
Privately printed, New York, 1966. 24 pp.

90 Giraudier, Antonio
*SELECTIONS FROM FIVE WORKS**
Adams Press, New York, 1968. 54 pp. $3.00

91 Guillén, Nicolás *Cuba*
*CUBA LIBRE, POEMS**
Translated by Langston Hughes and Ben Carruthers
Anderson and Ritchie, Los Angeles, 1948. 98 pp.
(selections from *El son entero*)

92 Hatchette, Wilfred I. *St Thomas*
*YOUTH'S FLIGHT; A COLLECTION OF POEMS**
The Art Shop, St. Thomas, 1928. 38 pp.

93 Hazell, Vivian *British West Indies*
*POEMS**
Arthur Stockwell, Ilfracombe, Devon, U.K., 1956. 30 pp.

94 Hendriks, A. L. *Jamaica*
*ON THIS MOUNTAIN AND OTHER POEMS**
Transatlantic Arts, New York, 1966. 59 pp. $4.00

95 Heredia, José María de *Cuba*
*THE TROPHIES; SONNETS**
Translated by Frank Sewall
Small, Maynard and Co., Boston, 1900. 133 pp.
(original title: *Los trofeos*)

96 Heredia, José María de
SONNETS OF JOSÉ MARÍA DE HEREDIA*
Translated by Edward Robeson Taylor
W. Doxey, San Francisco, 1900. 172 pp.
(selections from *Los trofeos*)

97 Heredia, José María de
SONNETS FROM THE TROPHIES OF
JOSE MARIA DE HEREDIA*
Translated by Edward Robeson Taylor
P. Elder and Co., San Francisco, 1906. 176 pp.
(selections from *Los trofeos*)

98 Heredia, José María de
TRANSLATIONS FROM JOSÉ MARÍA DE HEREDIA*
Translated by Merle St. Croix Wright
H. Vinal, Ltd., New York, 1927. 122 pp.

99 Heredia, José María de
THE TROPHIES WITH OTHER SONNETS*
Translated by John Myers O'Hara and John Hervey
The John Day Co., New York, 1929. 242 pp.
(original title: *Los trofeos*)

100 Heredia, José María de
TROPHIES*
Translated and introduced by Brian Hill
Dufour, Philadelphia, 1962. 73 pp. $3.50
(original title: *Los trofeos*)

101 Hernández Cruz, Victor *Puerto Rico*
SNAPS; POEMS
Vintage Books (Random House), New York, 1969. 135 pp. $4.95,
    $1.95 (paper)
(originally written in English)

102 Hill, Valdemar A. *St. Thomas*
RIPPLES*
The Art Shop, St. Thomas, 1935. 33 pp.

103 Jarvis, José Antonio *St. Thomas*
*FRUITS IN PASSING**
Jarvis Art Gallery, Charlotte Amalie, 1932. 99 pp.

104 Jarvis, José Antonio
*BAMBOULA DANCE AND OTHER POEMS**
The Art Shop, St. Thomas, 1935. 57 pp.

105 Jarvis, José Antonio
*BLUEBEARD'S LAST WIFE**
Jarvis Art Gallery, Charlotte Amalie, 1951. 25 pp.

106 Jones, Barbara Althea *Trinidad*
*AMONG THE POTATOES; A COLLECTION OF
   MODERN VERSE**
Arthur Stockwell, Ilfracombe, Devon, U.K., 1967. 96 pp.

107 Jones, Evan *Jamaica*
UNDERSTANDING; POEMS
Cambridge University Press, New York, 1968. 70 pp. $3.75 (paper)

108 Lambert, Calvin Stollmeyer *Trinidad*
*POEMS OF THE WEST INDIAN**
"Poetry of Today", London, 1938. 35 pp.

109 Lambert, Calvin Stollmeyer
*SELECTED POEMS OF A WEST INDIAN**
The Fortune Press, London, 1940. 58 pp.

110 La Rose, Anthony *Jamaica*
*FOUNDATIONS: A BOOK OF POEMS**
New Beacon Publications, London, 1966. 51 pp. 10s.

111 Laviaux, Léon *Martinique*
*THE EBON MUSE, AND OTHER POEMS**
Translated by John Myers O'Hara
Smith and Sale, Portland, 1914. 51 pp.
(original title not available)

112 Lee, Erica B. *St. Thomas*
REFLECTIONS; A COLLECTION OF POEMS*
Padilla Printing Works, San Juan, 1939. 50 pp.

113 Lee de Muñoz-Marín, Muna *Puerto Rico*
SEA-CHANGE*
The Macmillan Company, New York, 1923. 76 pp.
(Originally written in English)

114 Levy, Wesley *Jamaica*
THE MORNING STAR
Arthur Stockwell, Ilfracombe, Devon, U.K., 1964. 35 pp. 3s 6d

115 Lucie-Smith, Edward *Jamaica*
A TROPICAL CHILDHOOD, AND OTHER POEMS*
Oxford University Press, New York, 1961. 44 pp.

116 Lucie-Smith, Edward
CONFESSIONS AND HISTORIES
Oxford University Press, New York, 1964. 51 pp. $2.60

117 Lucie-Smith, Edward
BORROWED EMBLEMS*
Turret Books, London, 1967. 32 pp.

118 Lucie-Smith, Edward
THE LIVERPOOL SCENE
Doubleday, Garden City, 1968. 80 pp. $1.95 (paper)

119 Lucie-Smith, Edward
SNOW POEM*
Turret Books, London, 1968. 16 pp.

120 Lucie-Smith, Edward
TOWARDS SILENCE
Oxford University Press, New York, 1968. 62 pp. $1.75 (paper)

121 Lucie-Smith, Edward
EGYPTIAN ODE
Daedalus Press, London, 1969. 16 pp.

122 Lynch, Charles Anthony *Trinidad*
*GLADYS KLYNE, AND MORE HARMONY**
The Gorham Press, Boston, 1915. 75 pp.

123 Lyons, Miriam *Jamaica*
*FUGITIVE POEMS**
Unicorn Press, London, 1933. 54 pp.

124 McFarland, Harry Stanley *Jamaica*
EXPERIENCES OF A HEART, ITS JOYS,
*ITS SORROWS**
Meador Publishing Co., Boston, 1931. 68 pp.

125 McFarland, Harry Stanley
*PASSING THROUGH; A COLLECTION OF POEMS**
Wendell Malliet and Co., New York, 1950. 120 pp.

126 McFarland, Harry Stanley
*GROWING UP; A BOOK OF VERSE**
Meador Publishing Co., Boston, 1956. 88 pp.

127 McFarlane, John E. C. *Jamaica*
DAPHNĖ; A TALE OF THE HILLS OF ST. ANDREW,
*JAMAICA**
F. Wright, London, 1931. 93 pp.

128 McKay, Claude *Jamaica*
*CONSTAB BALLADS**
Watts and Co., London, 1912. 94 pp.

129 McKay, Claude
*SPRING IN NEW HAMPSHIRE AND OTHER POEMS**
Grant Richards, London, 1920. 40 pp.

130 McKay, Claude
*HARLEM: NEGRO METROPOLIS**
E. P. Dutton, New York, 1940. 262 pp.

131 McKay, Claude
*HARLEM SHADOWS**
Harcourt, Brace and World, New York, 1922. 95 pp.

132 McKay, Claude
*SELECTED POEMS**
Bookman Associates, New York, 1953. 112 pp.

133 McKay, Claude
SELECTED POEMS OF CLAUDE McKAY
Twayne, New York, 1953. 112 pp. $4.00

134 McKay, Claude
SELECTED POEMS
Harcourt, Brace and World, New York, 1969. 110 pp. $1.65 (paper)

135 McKay, Claude
SONGS OF JAMAICA
Mnemosyne Publishing Co., Miami, 1969. 140 pp. $6.75

136 MacKenzie, Rhoda *Jamaica*
JAMAICA POCOMANIA
MacLellan, Glasgow, 1969. 40 pp. 10s 6d, 7s 6d (paper)

137 Maraj, Jagdip *Trinidad*
THE FLAMING CIRCLE
McGill University Press, Montreal, 1966. 35 pp.

138 Margetson, George Reginald *St. Kitts*
ENGLAND IN THE WEST INDIES;
 *A NEGLECTED AND DEGENERATING EMPIRE**
Privately published, Cambridge, 1906. 35 pp.

139 Margetson, George Reginald
ETHIOPIA'S FLIGHT; THE NEGRO QUESTION,
 *OR THE WHITE MAN'S FEAR**
Privately published, Cambridge, 1907. 21 pp.

140 Margetson, George Reginald
*SONGS OF LIFE**
Sherman, French and Co., Boston, 1910. 57 pp.

141 Margetson, George Reginald
*THE FLEDGLING BARD AND THE POETRY SOCIETY**
R. G. Badger, Boston, 1916. 111 pp.

142 Marson, Una *Jamaica*
TOWARDS THE STARS; POEMS*
University of London Press, London, 1945. 63 pp.

143 Mead, Stella *Jamaica*
SPLENDOR AT DAWN—POEMS*
University of London Press, London, 1943. 35 pp.

144 Michael, Julia Warner *Bahamas*
NATIVE NASSAU: A MEMORY OF
* NEW PROVIDENCE ISLAND (POEMS)**
H. Marchbank's Print Shop, New York, 1909. 12 pp.

145 Nicholas, Arthur E. *Jamaica*
ARCADIA: POEMS*
Books for Today, Ltd., London, 1949. 108 pp.

146 Norman, Alma *Jamaica*
BALLADS OF JAMAICA
Longmans, Green and Co., London, 1967. 35 pp. 4s 6d

147 Ormsby, Harriet *Jamaica*
IDEAL JAMAICA AND OTHER POEMS*
Arthur Stockwell, Ltd., London, no date. 24 pp.

148 Paiewonsky, Isidor *St. Thomas*
CROUCHER BY THE FIRE*
Galleon Press, New York, 1933. 63 pp.

149 Richards, Edward A. *St. Thomas*
SHADOWS*
The Reflector, St. Thomas, 1933. 20 pp.

150 Roberts, W. Adolphe *Jamaica*
PIERROT WOUNDED AND OTHER POEMS*
Britton Publishing Co., New York, 1919. 87 pp.

151 Roberts, W. Adolphe
PANS AND PEACOCKS (POEMS)*
Four Seas Company, Boston, 1928. 80 pp.

152 St. John-Perse, Aléxis (pseud. of Aléxis Saint-Léger
Leger) *Guadeloupe*
*ANABASIS**
Translated by T. S. Eliot (bilingual edition)
Harcourt, New York, 1949. 109 pp.
(original title: *Anabase*)

153 St. John-Perse, Aléxis
*EXILE AND OTHER POEMS**
Translated by Denis Devlin (bilingual edition)
Pantheon Books, New York, 1949. 166 pp.
(original title: *Exile*)

154 St. John-Perse, Aléxis
*WINDS**
Translated by Hugh Chisolm (bilingual edition)
Pantheon Books, New York, 1953. 252 pp.
(original title: *Vents*)

155 St. John-Perse, Aléxis
*ÉLOGES AND OTHER POEMS**
Translated by Louis Varèse (bilingual edition)
Pantheon Books, New York, 1956. 103 pp.
(original tilte: *Éloges*)

156 St. John-Perse, Aléxis
*SEAMARKS**
Translated by Wallace Fowlie (bilingual edition)
Pantheon Books, New York, 1958. 363 pp.
(original title: *Amers*)

157 St. John-Perse, Aléxis
*CHRONIQUE**
Translated by Robert Fitzgerald (bilingual edition)
Pantheon Books, New York, 1961. 60 pp.
(original title: *Chronique*)

158 St. John-Perse, Aléxis
*BIRDS**
Translated by Robert Fitzgerald (bilingual edition)
Pantheon Books, New York, 1966. 71 pp.
(original title: *L'Ordre des oiseaux*)

159 St. John-Perse, Aléxis
*BIRDS**
Translated by J. Roger Little
North Gate Press, Durham, 1967. 19 pp.
(original title: *L'Ordre des oiseaux*)

160 Simpson, Louis *Jamaica*
*THE ARRIVISTES: POEMS 1940–49**
Fine Edition Press, New York, 1952. 93 pp.

161 Simpson, Louis
A DREAM OF GOVERNORS; POEMS
Wesleyan University Press, Middletown, 1959. 87 pp. $4.00, $2.00
  (paper)

162 Simpson, Louis
AT THE END OF THE OPEN ROAD
Wesleyan University Press, Middletown, 1963. 70 pp. $4.00, $2.00
  (paper)

163 Simpson, Louis
SELECTED POEMS
Harcourt, Brace and World, New York, 1965. 145 pp. $1.45 (paper)

164 Sookhdeo, Jaikissoon *Guyana*
*LET NOT THE GREAT**
Arthur Stockwell, Ilfracombe, Devon, U.K., 1964. 35 pp.

165 Todman, Gerwyn *St. Thomas*
*ST. THOMAS: A RETROSPECTION**
George E. Audain, Printer, St. Thomas, 1921. 58 pp.

166 Tree, Iris *Bahamas*
*POEMS**
John Lane, New York, 1919. 144 pp.

167 Tree, Iris
*THE TRAVELLER AND OTHER POEMS**
Boni and Liveright, New York, 1927. 89 pp.

168 *Tropica* (pseud. of Mary Adella Wolcott) *Jamaica*
THE ISLAND OF SUNSHINE*
Knickerbocker Press, New York, c1904. 55 pp.

169 Walcott, Derek *St. Lucia*
SELECTED POEMS
Farrar, Straus, and Giroux, New York, 1964. 85 pp. $4.95

170 Walcott, Derek
IN THE GREEN NIGHT; POEMS 1948–1960
Jonathan Cape Ltd., London, 1969. 79 pp. 8s. (paper)

171 Walcott, Derek
THE CASTAWAY AND OTHER POEMS
Jonathan Cape Ltd., London, 1969. 64 pp. 8s. (paper)

172 Walcott, Derek
THE GULF
Farrar, Straus and Giroux, New York, 1970. 111 pp. $5.50, $1.95
  (paper)

173 Wheeler, L. Richmond *Jamaica*
DESERT MUSINGS: VERSE*
Arthur Stockwell, London, 1920. 32 pp. 2s.

Short Stories

174 Anderson, Alston *Jamaica*
LOVERMAN*
Doubleday, Garden City, 1959. 177 pp.

175 Anthony, Michael *Trinidad*
MICHAEL ANTHONY'S TALES FOR
  YOUNG AND OLD*
Arthur Stockwell, Ilfracombe, Devon, U.K., 1967. 194 pp.

176 Blanco, Tomás *Puerto Rico*
THE CHILD'S GIFTS; A TWELFTH NIGHT TALE*
Translated by Harriet de Onís (bilingual edition)
Pan American Book Co., San Juan, 1954. 33 pp.
(original title: *Los aguinaldos del infante; glosa de la Epifanía*)

177 Carpentier, Alejo *Cuba*
WAR OF TIME
Translated by Frances Partridge
Knopf, New York, 1970. 192 pp. $4.95
(original title: *Guerra del tiempo*)

178 Cousins, Phyllis *Jamaica*
QUEEN OF THE MOUNTAIN
Ginn and Co., London, 1967. 48 pp. 3s 6d

179 Fariña, Richard *Cuba*
LONG TIME COMING AND A LONG TIME GONE
Random House, New York, 1969. 268 pp. $4.95
(a selection of short stories and some poetry)
(originally written in English)

180 McKay, Claude *Jamaica*
GINGERTOWN*
Harper and Bros., New York, 1932. 274 pp.

181 Naipaul, V. S. *Trinidad*
MIGUEL STREET
Vanguard Press, New York, 1960. 222 pp. $3.95 (paper)

182 Naipaul, V. S.
FLAG ON THE ISLAND
Macmillan, New York, 1968. 235 pp. $5.95

183 Rhys, Jean *Dominica*
THE LEFT BANK AND OTHER STORIES*
Jonathan Cape Ltd., London, 1947. 256 pp.

184 Rhys, Jean
TIGERS ARE BETTER LOOKING, WITH A
  SELECTION FROM THE LEFT BANK; STORIES
André Deutsch, London, 1968. 236 pp. 25s.

185 Rodriguez Escudero, Nestor A. *Puerto Rico*
LITORAL. SHORT STORIES OF THE SEA OF
  PUERTO RICO
Translated by Louise Florea Sweetman
Vantage Press, New York, 1969. 138 pp. $3.75
(original title: *Litoral. Cuentos del mar de Puerto Rico*)

186 St. Johnston, Thomas Reginald *Jamaica*
A WEST INDIAN PEPPER-POT;
  OR THIRTEEN 'QUASHIE' STORIES*
P. Allan and Co., London, 1928. 209 pp.

187 Sherlock, Philip M. *Jamaica*
IGUANA'S TAIL:
  CRICK CRACK STORIES FROM THE CARIBBEAN
T. Y. Crowell Co., New York, 1969. 97 pp. $3.95

188 Walrond, Eric *Guyana*
TROPIC DEATH*
Boni and Liveright, New York, 1926. 283 pp.

Novels

189 Aarons, R. L. C. *Jamaica*
ADELAIDE LINDSAY*
Cox (Bros.) and Wyman, London, 1944. 205 pp.

190 Abrahams, Peter *Jamaica*
DARK TESTAMENT*
Allen and Unwin, London, 1942. 160 pp.

191 Abrahams, Peter
THE PATH OF THUNDER*
Harper and Bros., New York, 1948. 278 pp.

192 Abrahams, Peter
WILD CONQUEST
Harper and Bros., New York, 1950. 309 pp. (out of print)
Faber and Faber, London, 1951. 15s.

193 Abrahams, Peter
RETURN TO GOLI
Faber and Faber, London, 1953. 224 pp. 12s 6d

194 Abrahams, Peter
MINE BOY*
Knopf, New York, 1955. 252 pp.

195 Abrahams, Peter
A WREATH FOR UDOMO
Knopf, New York, 1956. 356 pp. (out of print)
Faber and Faber, London, 1965. 309 pp. 6s 6d (paper)

196 Abrahams, Peter
NIGHT OF THEIR OWN
Knopf, New York, 1965. 237 pp. $4.95

197 Abrahams, Peter
TELL FREEDOM
Knopf, New York, 1966. 370 pp. $4.95

198 Abrahams, Peter
THIS ISLAND NOW
Knopf, New York, 1967. 305 pp. $5.95

199 Allfrey, Phyllis Shand *Dominica*
THE ORCHID HOUSE*
E. P. Dutton, New York, 1954. 223 pp.

200 Anthony, Michael *Trinidad*
MEN NEED SYMPATHY;
  A TALE OF FAMILY LIFE WITH JUST A LITTLE
  BLACKMAIL AND ONLY A MODICUM OF
  MURDER*
Methuen, London, 1943. 249 pp.

201 Anthony, Michael
GREEN DAYS BY THE RIVER
Houghton-Mifflin, Boston, 1967. 192 pp. $4.50

202 Anthony, Michael
THE GAMES WERE COMING
Houghton-Mifflin, Boston, 1968. 192 pp. $3.95

203 Anthony, Michael
THE YEAR IN SAN FERNANDO
Humanities Press, New York, 1970. 208 pp. $1.50 (paper)

204 Arcocha, Juan *Cuba*
A CANDLE IN THE WIND
Anonymous translation
Lyle Stuart, New York, 1967. 187 pp. $4.00
(original title not available)

205 Arenal, Humberto *Cuba*
THE SUN BEATS DOWN*
Translated by Joseph M. Bernstein
Hill and Wang, New York, 1959. 96 pp. $1.50
(original title: *El sol a plomo*)

206 Barrett, Lindsay *Jamaica*
SONG FOR MUMU
Longmans, Green and Co., London, 1967. 154 pp. 25s.

207 Barrett, Nathan *Jamaica*
BARS OF ADAMANT
Fleet Publishing Corporation, New York, 1966. 287 pp. $5.95

208 Bennett, Alvin *Jamaica*
GOD THE STONEBREAKER*
William Heinemann Ltd., London, 1964. 247 pp. 21s.

209 Braithwaite, Edward R. *Guyana*
TO SIR WITH LOVE
Prentice-Hall, Englewood Cliffs, 1960. 216 pp. $4.95

210 Braithwaite, Edward R.
A KIND OF HOMECOMING*
Prentice-Hall, Englewood Cliffs, 1962. 243 pp.

211 Braithwaite, Edward R.
CHOICE OF STRAWS
Bobbs-Merrill, Indianapolis, 1967. 198 pp. $4.00

212 Braithwaite, Edward R.
PAID SERVANT
McGraw-Hill, New York, 1968. 224 pp. $4.95

213 Campbell, George *Jamaica*
CRY FOR HAPPY*
Harcourt, Brace and World, New York, 1958. 246 pp.

214 Carew, Jan *Guyana*
A TOUCH OF MIDAS*
Coward-McCann, New York, 1958. 288 pp. $3.75
(original title: *Black Midas*)

215 Carew, Jan
THE WILD COAST*
Secker and Warburg, London, 1958, 256 pp.

216 Carew, Jan
THE LAST BARBARIAN*
Secker and Warburg, London, 1961. 286 pp. 6s.

217 Carpentier, Alejo *Cuba*
LOST STEPS
Translated by Harriet de Onís
Knopf, New York, 1956 and 1967. 307 pp. $5.95
(original title: *Los pasos perdidos*)

218 Carpentier, Alejo
THE KINGDOM OF THIS WORLD*
Translated by Harriet de Onís
Knopf, New York, 1957. 150 pp. $3.00
(original title: *El reino de este mundo*)

219 Carpentier, Alejo
EXPLOSION IN THE CATHEDRAL*
Translated by John Sturrock
Little, Brown and Co., Boston, 1963. 351 pp.
(original title: *El siglo de las luces*)

220 Chapman, Esther Hyman *Jamaica*
A STUDY IN BRONZE: A NOVEL OF JAMAICA*
Chantry, London, 1952. 249 pp.

221 Chapman, Esther Hyman
TOO MUCH SUMMER, A NOVEL OF JAMAICA*
Chantry, London, 1953. 190 pp

222 Chauvet, Marie *Haiti*
DANCE ON THE VOLCANO*
Translated by Salvator Attanasio
Sloane, New York, 1959. 376 pp. $4.50
(original title: *La danse sur le volcan*)

223 Clarke, Austin C. *Barbados*
THE SURVIVORS OF THE CROSSING*
William Heinemann Ltd., London, 1964. 202 pp. 18s.

224 Clarke, Austin C.
AMONG THE THISTLES AND THORNS*
William Heinemann Ltd., London, 1965. 192 pp. 21s.

225 Clarke, Austin C.
*THE MEETING POINT**
William Heinemann Ltd., London, 1967. 249 pp. 30s.

226 Dathorne, Oscar R. *Guyana*
*DUMPLINGS IN THE SOUP**
Cassell, London, 1963. 192 pp.

227 Dathorne, Oscar R,
*THE SCHOLAR MAN**
Cassell, London, 1964. 180 pp. 16s.

228 Dawes, Neville *Jamaica*
*THE LAST ENCHANTMENT**
MacGibbon and Kee, London, 1962. 288 pp.

229 De Boissiere, Ralph *Trinidad*
*CROWN JEWEL**
Australasian Book Society, Melbourne, 1952. 432 pp.

230 De Boissiere, Ralph
*RUM AND COCA-COLA**
Australasian Book Society, Melbourne, 1956. 313 pp.

231 De Boissiere, Ralph
*NO SADDLES FOR KANGAROOS, A NOVEL**
Australasian Book Society, Melbourne, 1964. 316 pp.

232 De Lisser, Herbert G. *Jamaica*
*JANE'S CAREER; A STORY OF JAMAICA**
Methuen, London, 1914. 311 pp.

233 De Lisser, Herbert G.
*SUSAN PROUDLEIGH**
Methuen, London, 1915. 309 pp.

234 De Lisser, Herbert G.
*UNDER THE SUN: A JAMAICAN COMEDY**
E. Benn, London, 1937. 269 pp.

235 De Lisser, Herbert G.
*PSYCHE**
E. Benn, London, 1952. 224 pp.

236 De Lisser, Herbert G.
*MORGAN'S DAUGHTER**
E. Benn, London, 1953. 220 pp.

237 De Lisser, Herbert G.
*THE WHITE WITCH OF ROSE HALL**
E. Benn, London, 1955. 255 pp.

238 De Lisser, Herbert G.
*THE CUP AND THE LIP, A ROMANCE**
E. Benn, London, 1956. 256 pp.

239 Desnoes, Edmundo *Cuba*
*INCONSOLABLE MEMORIES**
Translated by the author
New American Library, New York, 1967. 155 pp. $4.50
(original title not available)

240 Drayton, Geoffrey *Barbados*
*CHRISTOPHER (A NOVEL OF CHILDHOOD IN
    THE WEST INDIES)**
Collins, London, 1959. 192 pp. 13s 6d

241 Drayton, Geoffrey
*ZOHARA**
Secker and Warburg, London, 1961. 185 pp. 7s 6d

242 DuQuesnay, Frederick J. Le Mercier *Jamaica*
*A PRINCESS FOR PORT ROYAL;
    A ROMANTIC NOVEL**
Arthur Stockwell, Ilfracombe, Devon, U.K., 1960. 158 pp.

243 Ellington, Richard *St. John*
*IT'S A CRIME**
William Morrow and Co., New York, 1948. 243 pp.

244 Ellington, Richard
*SHOOT THE WORKS**
William Morrow and Co., New York, 1948. 249 pp.

245 Ellington, Richard
*STONE COLD DEAD**
William Morrow and Co., New York, 1950. 247 pp.

246 Ellington, Richard
*EXIT FOR A DAME**
William Morrow and Co., New York, 1951. 246 pp.

247 Ellington, Richard
*JUST KILLING TIME**
William Morrow and Co., New York, 1953. 219 pp.

248 Emtage, J. B. *Barbados*
*BROWN SUGAR, A VESTIGIAL TALE**
Collins, London, 1966. 128 pp. 18s.

249 Fariña, Richard *Cuba*
BEEN DOWN SO LONG IT LOOKS UP TO ME
Random House, New York, 1966. 329 pp. $5.95
(originally written in English)

250 Ferguson, Merrill *Jamaica*
VILLAGE OF LOVE
MacGibbon and Kee, London, 1960. 270 pp. $5.00

251 Fraser, Fitzroy *Jamaica*
*WOUNDS IN THE FLESH**
New Authors, London, 1962. 189 pp. 16s.

252 Gaillard, Robert *Martinique*
*MARIE OF THE ISLES**
Translated by Merle Severy
A. A. Wyn, New York, 1953. 422 pp. $3.50
(original title: *Marie des isles*)

253 Galván, Manuel de Jesús *Dominican Republic*
THE CROSS AND THE SWORD*
Translated by Robert Graves
Indiana University Press, Bloomington, 1954. 366 pp.
(original title: *Enriquillo, leyenda histórica dominicana*)

254 Gimble, Rosemary *Guyana*
JONATHAN AND LARGE*
André Deutsch, London, 1965. 88 pp.

255 Glissant, Edouard *French West Indies*
THE RIPENING
Translated by Frances Frenaye
G. Braziller, New York, 1959. 253 pp. $4.50
(original title: *La lézarde*)

256 Grange, Peter *Jamaica*
KING CREOLE*
Jarrolds, London, 1966. 287 pp.

257 Guy, Rosa *Trinidad*
BIRD AT MY WINDOW*
Souvenir Press, London, 1966. 282 pp.

258 Hamilton, Bruce *Jamaica*
TOO MUCH OF WATER*
Cresset Press, London, 1958. 271 pp.

259 Harris, Wilson *Guyana*
THE FAR JOURNEY OF OUDIN
Faber and Faber, London, 1961. 136 pp. 15s.

260 Harris, Wilson
THE WHOLE ARMOUR
Faber and Faber, London, 1962. 128 pp. 16s.

261 Harris, Wilson
THE SECRET LADDER
Faber and Faber, London, 1963. 127 pp. 16s.

262 Harris, Wilson
HEARTLAND
Faber and Faber, London, 1964. 96 pp. 16s.

263 Harris, Wilson
THE EYE OF THE SCARECROW
Faber and Faber, London, 1965. 108 pp. 16s.

264 Harris, Wilson
THE WAITING ROOM
Faber and Faber, London, 1967. 80 pp. 18s.

265 Harris, Wilson
TUMATUMARI
Faber and Faber, London, 1968. 156 pp. 25s.

266 Harris, Wilson
PALACE OF THE PEACOCK
Faber and Faber, London, 1969. 156 pp. 9s. (paper)

267 Harris, Wilson
ASCENT TO OMAI
Faber and Faber, London, 1970. 128 pp. 25s.

268 Hearne, John *Jamaica*
VOICES UNDER THE WINDOW*
Faber and Faber, London, 1955. 163 pp. 10s 6d

269 Hearne, John
STRANGER AT THE GATE*
Faber and Faber, London, 1956. 304 pp. 15s.

270 Hearne, John
THE FACES OF LOVE
Faber and Faber, London, 1957. 267 pp. 15s.

271 Hearne, John
THE EYE OF THE STORM*
Little, Brown and Co., Boston, 1958. 328 pp. $4.00

272 Hearne, John
THE AUTUMN EQUINOX
Vanguard Press, New York, 1961. 272 pp. $3.95

273 Hearne, John
THE LAND OF THE LIVING
Harper and Row, New York, 1962. 280 pp. (out of print)
Faber and Faber, London, 1961. 280 pp. 18s.

274 Hercules, Frank *Trinidad*
*WHERE THE HUMMING-BIRD FLIES**
Harcourt, Brace and World, New York, 1961. 212 pp. $3.95

275 Hercules, Frank
I WANT A BLACK DOLL
Simon and Schuster, New York, 1967. 320 pp. $5.95

276 Hodge, Merle
CRICK CRACK MONKEY
André Deutsch, London, 1970. 160 pp. 30s.

277 Hutchinson, Lionel *Barbados*
MAN FROM THE PEOPLE
William Collins Sons and Co., London, 1970. 256 pp. 30s.

278 Iremonger, Lucille *Jamaica*
*CREOLE**
Hutchinson and Co., London, 1951. 234 pp. 9s 6d

279 Iremonger, Lucille
*THE CANNIBALS, A NOVEL**
Hammond, Hammond and Co., London, 1952. 254 pp.

280 Iremonger, Lucille
*YES MY DARLING DAUGHTER**
Secker and Warburg, London, 1964. 218 pp.

281 James, Cyril L. R. *Trinidad*
*MINTY ALLEY**
Secker and Warburg, London, 1936. 320 pp.

282 James, Cyril L. R.
THE BLACK JACOBINS*
Vintage Books, New York, 1963. 426 pp.

283 Khan, Ismith *Trinidad*
THE JUMBLE BIRD
Ivan Obolensky, New York, 1963. 224 pp. $3.95

284 Khan, Ismith
THE OBEAH MAN*
Hutchinson and Co., London, 1964. 192 pp. 18s.

285 Kizerman, Rudolph *Barbados*
STAND UP IN THE WORLD
Blackbird Books, London, 1968. 198 pp. $2.35 (paper)

286 Labarthe, P. J. *Puerto Rico*
MARY SMITH*
Whittier Books, New York, 1958. 311 pp.
(originally written in English)

287 La Fortune, Knolly S. *Trinidad*
*LEGEND OF T-MARIE; A TALE OF
    TRINIDAD FOLKLORE**
Privately printed, London, 1968. 128 pp.

288 Laguerre, Enrique A. *Puerto Rico*
THE LABYRINTH*
Translated by William Rose
Las Americas, New York, 1960. 275 pp.
(original title: *El laberinto*)

289 Lamming, George *Barbados*
IN THE CASTLE OF MY SKIN (1950)
Macmillan, New York, 1970. 303 pp. $1.50 (paper)

290 Lamming, George
THE EMIGRANTS*
McGraw-Hill, New York, 1955. 282 pp. $3.75

291 Lamming, George
OF AGE AND INNOCENCE
Michael Joseph, London, 1958. 413 pp. 21s.

292 Lamming, George
SEASON OF ADVENTURE*
Michael Joseph, London, 1960. 367 pp. 21s.

293 Lauchmonen (pseud. of Peter Kempadoo) *Guyana*
OLD THOM'S HARVEST*
Eyre and Spottiswoode, London, 1965. 195 pp.

294 Lauchmonen
GUIANA BOY*
New Literature Ltd., Crawley, Sussex, U.K., 1960. 172 pp.

295 Lima, Clara Rosa de *Trinidad*
TOMORROW WILL ALWAYS COME*
Ivan Obolensky, New York, 1965. 277 pp. $4.50

296 Lockett, Mary F. *Jamaica*
CHRISTOPHER (A NOVEL)*
The Abbey Press, New York, 1902. 328 pp.

297 Lovelace, Earl *Tobago*
WHILE GODS ARE FALLING
Henry Regnery, Chicago, 1966. 255 pp. $4.95

298 Lovelace, Earl
THE SCHOOLMASTER
Henry Regnery, Chicago, 1968. 224 pp. $4.95

299 McDonald, Ian *Trinidad*
THE HUMMING-BIRD TREE
William Heinemann, Ltd., London, 1969. 181 pp. 30s

300 McKay, Claude *Jamaica*
HOME TO HARLEM (1928)
Pocket Books (Simon and Schuster), New York, 1965. 180 pp. $0.50
  (paper)

301 McKay, Claude
*BANJO, A STORY WITHOUT A PLOT**
Harper and Bros., New York, 1929. 326 pp.

302 McKay, Claude
*BANANA BOTTOM** (*1933*)
Harper and Row, New York, 1969. 317 pp. $1.60 (paper)

303 Mais, Roger *Jamaica*
*THE HILLS WERE JOYFUL TOGETHER**
Jonathan Cape Ltd., London, 1953. 288 pp. 12s 6d

304 Mais, Roger
*BROTHER MAN**
Jonathan Cape Ltd., London, 1954. 191 pp.

305 Mais, Roger
*BLACK LIGHTNING**
Jonathan Cape Ltd., London, 1955, 222 pp.

306 Mais, Roger
THE THREE NOVELS OF ROGER MAIS
Jonathan Cape Ltd., London, 1966. 700 pp. 35s.

307 Maran, René *Martinique*
*BATOUALA**
Translated by Alvah C. Bessie
Limited Editions Club, New York, 1932. 117 pp.
(original title: *Batouala*)

308 Maran, René
BATOUALA
Translated by Adele Szold Seltzer
Kennikat Press, Port Washington, 1969. 207 pp. $7.50
(original title: *Batouala*)

309 Marr, Nancy *Jamaica*
*THE DARK DIVIDE: A ROMANCE**
Museum Press, London, 1951. 256 pp.

310 Marr, Nancy
ADAM*
Museum Press, London, 1952. 256 pp.

311 Marr, Nancy
NIGGER BROWN*
Museum Press, London, 1953. 256 pp.

312 Marshall, Paule *Jamaica*
SOUL CLAP HANDS AND SING*
Atheneum, New York, 1961. 177 pp.

313 Marshall, Paule
THE CHOSEN PLACE, THE TIMELESS PEOPLE
Harcourt, Brace and World, New York, 1969. 472 pp. $8.95

314 Marshall, Paule
BROWN GIRL, BROWNSTONES
Avon Books, New York, 1970. 256 pp. $0.95 (paper)

315 Marugg, Tip *Netherland Antilles*
WEEKEND PILGRIMAGE*
Translated by Roy Edwards
Hutchinson and Co., London, 1960. 192 pp. 15s.
(original title not available)

316 Mendes, Alfred H. *Trinidad*
PITCH LAKE*
Gerald Duckworth and Co., London, 1934. 352 pp.

317 Mendes, Alfred H.
BLACK FAUNS*
Gerald Duckworth and Co., London, 1935. 328 pp.

318 Mittelholzer, Edgar A. *Guyana*
A MORNING IN TRINIDAD*
Doubleday, Garden City, 1950. 250 pp.
(original title: *A Morning at the Office*)

319 Mittelholzer, Edgar A.
SHADOWS MOVE AMONG THEM*
Lippincott, Philadelphia, 1951. 331 pp.

320 Mittelholzer, Edgar A.
THE WEATHER IN MIDDENSHOT*
John Day, New York, 1953. 280 pp.

321 Mittelholzer, Edgar A.
THE LIFE AND DEATH OF SYLVIA*
John Day, New York, 1953. 316 pp. $4.00

322 Mittelholzer, Edgar A,
THE HARROWING OF HUBERTUS*
John Day, New York, 1955. 303 pp.

323 Mittelholzer, Edgar A.
MY BONES AND FLUTE*
Secker and Warburg, London, 1955. 222 pp.

324 Mittelholzer, Edgar A.
OF TREES AND THE SEA*
Secker and Warburg, London, 1956. 256 pp.

325 Mittelholzer, Edgar A.
A TALE OF THREE PLACES*
Secker and Warburg, London, 1957. 347 pp.

326 Mittelholzer, Edgar A.
THE MAD MACMULLOCHS*
Peter Owen Ltd., London, 1959. 234 pp.

327 Mittelholzer, Edgar A.
A TWINKLING IN THE TWILIGHT*
Secker and Warburg, London, 1959. 269 pp. 18s.

328 Mittelholzer, Edgar A.
THE WEATHER FAMILY
Secker and Warburg, London, 1959. 339 pp. $6.00

329 Mittelholzer, Edgar A.
*ELTONSBRODY**
Secker and Warburg, London, 1960. 191 pp. 7s 6d

330 Mittelholzer, Edgar A.
*LATTICED ECHOES: A NOVEL IN LEITMOTIV
    MANNER**
Secker and Warburg, London, 1960. 254 pp. 18s.

331 Mittelholzer, Edgar A.
CHILDREN OF KAYWANA
Secker and Warburg, London, 1952. 516 pp. 55s.

332 Mittelholzer, Edgar A.
*THE PILING OF CLOUDS**
Putnam and Co., London, 1961. 262 pp.

333 Mittelholzer, Edgar A.
*THUNDER RETURNING;
    A NOVEL IN LEITMOTIV MANNER*
Secker and Warburg, London, 1961. 240 pp. 25s.

334 Mittelholzer, Edgar A.
THE WOUNDED AND THE WORRIED
Putnam and Co., London, 1962. 224 pp. 16s.

335 Mittelholzer, Edgar A.
*UNCLE PAUL**
MacDonald and Co., London, 1963. 222 pp.

336 Mittelholzer, Edgar A.
*A MORNING AT THE OFFICE**
Penguin Books, Harmondsworth, U.K., 1964. 222 pp. 4s. (paper)

337 Mittelholzer, Edgar A.
*THE ALONENESS OF MRS. CHATHAM**
Tandem Books, London, 1965. 224 pp. 3s 6d (paper)

338 Mittelholzer, Edgar A.
SYLVIA
Four Square Books, London, 1968. 256 pp. 5s. (paper)

339 Mittelholzer, Edgar A.
THE JILKINGTON DRAMA*
Abelard-Schuman, New York, 1965. 190 pp.

340 Mittelholzer, Edgar A.
THE OLD BLOOD
Fawcett Crest paperback, New York, 1968. 416 pp. $0.95 (paper)
(original title: *Kaywana Blood*)

341 Mittelholzer, Edgar A.
CORENTYNE THUNDER
Humanities Press, New York, 1970. 234 pp. $1.50 (paper)

342 Morris, John (pseud. for Morris Cargill and John Hearne)
   Jamaica
FEVER GRASS
G. P. Putnam's, New York, 1969. 256 pp. $5.95

343 Morris, John
THE CANDYWINE DEVELOPMENT
William Collins Sons and Co., London, 1970. 288 pp. 30s.

344 Naipaul, V. S. *Trinidad*
THE MYSTIC MASSEUR
Vanguard Press, New York, 1959. 215 pp. $3.50

345 Naipaul, V. S.
MR. STONE AND THE KNIGHT'S COMPANION*
Macmillan, New York, 1964. 159 pp.

346 Naipaul, V. S.
AREA OF DARKNESS
Macmillan, New York, 1965. 282 pp. $5.95

347 Naipaul, V. S.
THE MIMIC MEN
Macmillan, New York, 1967. 301 pp. $5.95

348 Naipaul, V. S.
THE SUFFRAGE OF ELVIRA
André Deutsch, London, 1969. 240 pp. 25s.

349 Naipaul, V. S.
A HOUSE FOR MR. BISWAS
McGraw-Hill, New York, 1961. 531 pp.
Penguin Books. Harmondsworth, U.K., 1969. 592 pp. 10s. (paper)

350 Nicole, Christopher *Guyana*
OFF-WHITE
Jarrolds, London, 1959. 224 pp. 15s.

351 Nicole, Christopher
SHADOWS IN THE JUNGLE*
Jarrolds, London, 1961. 224 pp. 16s.

352 Nicole, Christopher
RATOON*
St. Martin's Press, New York, 1962. 256 pp. $4.50

353 Nicole, Christopher
DARK NOON*
Jarrolds, London, 1963. 240 pp. 18s.

354 Nicole, Christopher
AMYOT'S CAY*
Jarrolds, London, 1964. 256 pp. 18s.

355 Nicole, Christopher
BLOOD AMYOT*
Jarrolds, London, 1964. 256 pp. 21s.

356 Nicole, Christopher
THE AMYOT CRIME*
Jarrolds, London, 1965. 288 pp. 25s.

357 Nicole, Christopher
WHITE BOY*
Hutchinson and Co., London, 1966. 288 pp. 25s.

358 Nicole, Christopher
THE SELF LOVERS
William Heinemann Ltd., London, 1968. 256 pp. 25s. 11s. (paper)

359 Nicole, Christopher
THE THUNDER AND THE SHOUTING
Hutchinson and Co., London, 1969. 256 pp. 30s.

360 Nicole, Christopher
THE LONGEST PLEASURE
Hutchinson and Co., London, 1970. 256 pp. 30s.

361 Palmer, C. Everard *Jamaica*
THE CLOUD WITH THE SILVER LINING
Pantheon Books, New York, 1967. 164 pp. $3.95

362 Palmer, C. Everard
BIG DOC BITTEROOT*
André Deutsch, London, 1968. 160 pp. 16s.

363 Palmer, C. Everard
THE SUN SALUTES YOU
André Deutsch, London, 1970. 144 pp. 18s.

364 Patterson, H. Orlando *Jamaica*
THE CHILDREN OF SISYPHUS*
Houghton-Mifflin, Boston, 1965. 206 pp.

365 Patterson, H. Orlando
AN ABSENCE OF RUINS*
Hutchinson and Co., London, 1967. 160 pp.

366 Quayle, Ada *Jamaica*
THE MISTRESS*
MacGibbon and Kee, London, 1957. 303 pp.

367 Rasmussen, Emil Michael *Virgin Islands*
THE FIRST NIGHT*
Wendell Malliet Co., New York, 1947. 278 pp.

368 Reid, V. S. *Jamaica*
NEW DAY*
Knopf, New York, 1949. 374 pp.

369 Reid, V. S.
*THE LEOPARD**
Viking Press, New York, 1958. 159 pp.

370 Rhys, Jean *Dominica*
WIDE SARGASSO SEA
Norton, New York, 1967. 190 pp. $4.50

371 Rhys, Jean
VOYAGE IN THE DARK (1934)
Norton, New York, 1968. 188 pp. $4.95

372 Rhys, Jean
QUARTET
Simon and Schuster, New York, 1929. 228 pp.
André Deutsch, London, 1969. 186 pp. 25s.
(original title: *Postures*, 1928)

373 Rhys, Jean
AFTER LEAVING MR. MACKENZIE
Knopf, New York, 1931. 227 pp.
André Deutsch, London, 1969. 191 pp. 25s.

374 Rhys, Jean
GOOD MORNING, MIDNIGHT (1939)
Harper and Row, New York, 1970. 189 pp. $5.95

375 Richer, Clément *Martinique*
*TI-COYO AND HIS SHARK; AN IMMORAL FABLE**
Translated by Gerald Hopkins
Knopf, New York, 1951. 235 pp.
(original title: *Ti-Coyo et son requin*)

376 Richer, Clément
*SON OF TI-COYO**
Translated by Gerald Hopkins
Knopf, New York, 1954. 245 pp.
(original title: *Nouvelles aventures de Ti-Coyo et de son requin*)

377 Riera, Pepita *Cuba*
*PRODIGY**
Pageant Press, New York, 1956. 287 pp. $3.50
(original title: *El amor que no quisiste*)

378 Roberts, W. Adolphe *Jamaica*
*THE HAUNTING HAND**
Macaulay Co., New York, 1926. 309 pp.

379 Roberts, W. Adolphe
*THE MIND READER**
Macaulay Co., New York, 1929. 277 pp.

380 Roberts, W. Adolphe
*THE MORALIST**
Mohawk Press, New York, 1931. 300 pp.

381 Roberts, W. Adolphe
*THE TOP FLOOR KILLER**
Nicholson and Watson, London, 1935. 319 pp.

382 Roberts, W. Adolphe
*THE POMEGRANATE**
Bobbs-Merrill, New York, 1941. 313 pp.

383 Roberts, W. Adolphe
*ROYAL STREET, A NOVEL OF OLD NEW ORLEANS**
Bobbs-Merrill, New York, 1944. 324 pp.

384 Roberts, W. Adolphe
BRAVE MARDI GRAS,
   *A NEW ORLEANS NOVEL OF THE '60s**
Bobbs-Merrill, New York, 1946. 318 pp.

385 Roberts, W. Adolphe
CREOLE DUSK, A NEW ORLEANS NOVEL OF
   *THE '80s**
Bobbs-Merrill, New York, 1948. 325 pp.

386 Roberts, W. Adolphe
*THE SINGLE STAR, A NOVEL OF CUBA IN THE '90s**
Boobs-Merrill, New York, 1949. 378 pp.

387 Rogers, Joel Augustus *Jamaica*
*SHE WALKS IN BEAUTY**
Western Publishers, Los Angeles, 1963. 316 pp.

388 Roumain, Jacques *Haiti*
*MASTERS OF THE DEW**
Translated by Langston Hughes and Mercer Cook
Regnal and Hitchcock, New York, 1964. 180 pp.
(original title: *Gouveneurs de la rosée*)

389 Roy, Namba *Jamaica*
*BLACK ALBINO**
New Literature, London, 1961. 196 pp.

390 Saher, Lilla van *Curaçao*
*THE ECHO**
Anonymous translation
E. P. Dutton, New York, 1947. 260 pp.
(original title unavailable)

391 Saher, Lilla van
*MACAMBA**
Anonymous translation
E. P. Dutton, New York, 1949. 264 pp.
(original title unavailable)

392 St. Omer, Garth *St. Lucia*
A ROOM ON THE HILL
Faber and Faber, London, 1968. 190 pp. 25s.

393 St. Omer, Garth
SHADES OF GREY
Faber and Faber, London, 1968. 224 pp. 25s.

394 St. Omer, Garth
NOR ANY COUNTRY
Faber and Faber, London, 1969. 110 pp. 21s.

395 Salkey, Andrew *Jamaica*
*A QUALITY OF VIOLENCE**
New Authors Ltd., London, 1959. 205 pp. 15s.

396 Salkey, Andrew
*ESCAPE TO AN AUTUMN PAVEMENT**
Hutchinson and Co., London, 1960. 207 pp. 6s 6d

397 Salkey, Andrew
DROUGHT
Oxford University Press, London, 1966. 152 pp. 13s 6d

398 Salkey, Andrew
RIOT
Oxford University Press, London, 1967. 202 pp. 15s.

399 Salkey, Andrew
THE LATE EMANCIPATION OF JERRY STOVER
Hutchinson and Co., London, 1968. 245 pp. 11s.

400 Salkey, Andrew
THE ADVENTURES OF CATULLUS KELLY
Hutchinson and Co., London, 1969. 192 pp. 27s 6d

401 Salkey, Andrew
JONAH SIMPSON
Roy Publishers, New York, 1970. 168 pp. $4.95

402 Scott, Michael *Jamaica*
TOM CRINGLE'S LOG
E. P. Dutton, New York, 1969. $2.95

403 Selvon, Samuel *Trinidad*
*A BRIGHTER SUN**
Viking Press, New York, 1953. 215 pp.

404 Selvon, Samuel
*AN ISLAND IS A WORLD**
Allan Wingate, London, 1955. 288 pp.

405 Selvon, Samuel
*THE LONELY LONDONERS**
St. Martin's Press, New York, 1957. 171 pp. $2.95

406 Selvon, Samuel
WAYS OF SUNLIGHT
St. Martin's Press, New York, 1957. 188 pp.
MacGibbon and Kee, London, 1957. 188 pp. 18s.

407 Selvon, Samuel
*TURN AGAIN TIGER**
St. Martin's Press, New York, 1959. 246 pp. $3.95

408 Selvon, Samuel
*I HEAR THUNDER**
St. Martin's Press, New York, 1963. 192 pp.

409 Selvon, Samuel
*THE HOUSING LARK**
MacGibbon and Kee, London, 1965. 155 pp.

410 Selvon, Samuel
PLAINS OF CARONI
MacGibbon and Kee, London, 1970. 167 pp. 30s.

411 Sherlock, Philip M. *Jamaica*
ANANSI, THE SPIDER MAN
T. Y. Crowell Co., New York, 1954. 112 pp. $3.95

412 Sherlock, Philip M.
THREE FINGER JACK'S TREASURE
St. Martin's Press, New York, 1961. 176 pp. $2.95

413 Simpson, Louis *Jamaica*
*RIVERSIDE DRIVE**
Atheneum, New York, 1962. 303 pp.

414 Sobers, Gary *Barbados*
BONAVENTURE AND THE FLASHING BLADE
Pelham, London, 1967. 160 pp. 13s 6d

415 Tapia y Rivera, Alejandro *Puerto Rico*
*ENARDO AND ROSAEL; AN ALLEGORICAL NOVELLA**
Translated by Alejandro Tapia, Jr.
Philosophical Library, New York, 1952. 156 pp. $2.75
(original title: *Enardo y Rosael*)

416 Thoby-Marcelin, Philippe and Pierre Marcelin *Haiti*
*CANAPÉ-VERT**
Translated by Edward LaRocque Tinker
Farrar and Rinehart, New York, 1944. 225 pp.
(original title: *Canapé-vert*)

417 Thoby-Marcelin, Philippe and Pierre Marcelin
*THE BEAST OF THE HAITIAN HILLS**
Translated by Peter C. Rhodes
Rinehart and Co., New York, 1946. 213 pp.
(original title: *La bête du museau*)

418 Thoby-Marcelin, Philippe and Pierre Marcelin
*THE PENCIL OF GOD**
Translated by Leonard Thomas
Houghton-Mifflin, Boston, 1951. 204 pp.
(original title: *Le crayon de Dieu*)

419 Thoby-Marcelin, Philippe and Pierre Marcelin
ALL MEN ARE MAD
Translated by Eva Thoby-Marcelin
Farrar, Straus and Giroux, New York, 1970. 179 pp. $6.75
(original title: *Touts les hommes sont fous*)

420 Tomlinson, Frederick Charles *Jamaica*
THE HELIONS; OR, THE DEEDS OF RIO:
A POLITICAL COMEDY*
Simpkin, Marshall and Co., London, 1930. 343 pp.

421 Vestdijk, Simon *Netherland Antilles*
RUM ISLAND*
Translated by B. K. Bowes
John Calder, London, 1963. 376 pp.
(original title not available)

422 Villaverde, Cirilo *Cuba*
THE QUADROON OR CECILIA VALDÉS*
Translated by Mariano J. Lorente
Farrar, Straus and Giroux, New York, 1935. 399 pp.
(original title: *Cecilia Valdés o la loma del ángel*)

423 Villaverde, Cirilo
CECILIA VALDÉS, A NOVEL OF CUBAN CUSTOMS*
Translated by Sydney G. Gest
Vantage Press, New York, 1962. 546 pp.
(original title: *Cecilia Valdés o la loma del ángel*)

424 Ward, Lynd *Jamaica*
GOD'S MAN: A NOVEL IN WOODCUTS*
Harrison-Smith, New York, 1929. 185 pp.

425 Williams, Denis *Guyana*
OTHER LEOPARDS*
Hutchinson and Co., London, 1963. 222 pp.

426 Williams, Denis
THE THIRD TEMPTATION: A NOVEL
Calder and Boyars, London, 1968. 117 pp. 25s.

427 Wynter, Sylvia *Jamaica*
THE HILLS OF HEBRON*
Simon and Schuster, New York, 1962. 315 pp.

Indexes *Figures refer to item numbers*

AUTHORS

TITLES

ORIGINAL TITLES *(when not English)*

COUNTRIES